GOURAMIS AND
OTHER ANABANTOIDS

Ctenopoma nanum spawning.

by Hans-Joachim Richter

Measurement Conversion Factors

When you know—	Multiply by—	To find—
Length:		
Millimeters (mm)	0.04	inches (in)
Centimeters (cm)	0.4	inches (in)
Meters (m)	3.3	feet (ft)
Mass (Weight):		
Grams (g)	0.035	ounces (oz)
Kilograms (kg)	2.2	pounds (lb)
Volume:		
Milliliters (ml)	0.03	fluid ounces (fl oz)
Liters (L)	2.1	pints (pt)
Liters (L)	1.06	quarts (qt)
Liters (L)	0.26	U.S. gallons (gal)
Liters (L)	0.22	Imperial gallons (gal)
Cubic centimeters (cc)	16.387	cubic inches (cu in)
Temperature:		
Celsius (°C)	multiply by 1.8, add 32	Fahrenheit (°F)

Photos by the author unless credited otherwise.

Originally published as DAS BUCH DER
LABYRINTHFISCHE
by Neumann Verlag, Leipzig, DDR

© **1988 by T.F.H. Publications, Inc.**

Distributed in the UNITED STATES by T.F.H. Publications, Inc., One T.F.H. Plaza, Neptune City, NJ 07753; in CANADA to the Pet Trade by H & L Pet Supplies Inc., 27 Kingston Crescent, Kitchener, Ontario N2B 2T6; Rolf C. Hagen Ltd., 3225 Sartelon Street, Montreal 382 Quebec; in CANADA to the Book Trade by Macmillan of Canada (A Division of Canada Publishing Corporation), 164 Commander Boulevard, Agincourt, Ontario M1S 3C7; in ENGLAND by T.F.H. Publications Limited, Cliveden House/Priors Way/Bray, Maidenhead, Berkshire SL6 2HP, England; in AUSTRALIA AND THE SOUTH PACIFIC by T.F.H. (Australia) Pty. Ltd., Box 149, Brookvale 2100 N.S.W., Australia; in NEW ZEALAND by Ross Haines & Son, Ltd., 18 Monmouth Street, Grey Lynn, Auckland 2, New Zealand; in SINGAPORE AND MALAYSIA by MPH Distributors (S) Pte., Ltd., 601 Sims Drive, #03/07/21, Singapore 1438; in the PHILIPPINES by Bio-Research, 5 Lippay Street, San Lorenzo Village, Makati Rizal; in SOUTH AFRICA by Multipet Pty. Ltd., 30 Turners Avenue, Durban 4001. Published by T.F.H. Publications, Inc. Manufactured in the United States of America by T.F.H. Publications, Inc.

TABLE OF CONTENTS

Foreword

With increasing industrialization in many areas, man takes every opportunity to get a little closer to nature. The ever increasing numbers of visitors to zoological gardens, the numerous natural history films in the cinema and on television and the huge choice of appropriate literature are all signs that many people seek to bring nature of one sort or another into their own environment. The major part of our planet is covered with water. It is not surprising therefore, that many people are turning for pleasure to a little underwater world of their own while visitors to large public aquaria are presented with the bigger representatives of the fish world. There are aquarists in all countries who like to bring a smaller representation of aquatic life, particularly tropical, into their homes. It is easy to understand why numbers of aquarists are continually increasing. A display of fish is a good way of beautifying one's apartment.

Foreword

Hans Joachim Richter, the world's leading fish photographer and author of this book.

As the trees in the jungle are cleared, the earth runs off with the rains and makes the mighty rivers brown with mud, making normal breathing for fishes more and more difficult. This is a river in Uganda flowing into Lake Victoria. Photo by Herbert R. Axelrod.

Foreword

By observing their behavior, and breeding fish, the enthusiast is forever increasing his knowledge. The variety of form, color and behavior produces a fish for nearly every taste. The present trend is not only to keep certain varieties of animals, but to delve more and more for information on their natural behavior, biotopes and ecology.

In all parts of the world, technical literature is continually reporting new developments in the hobby of aquaristics, and thus encouraging further research. The quest for ever more specialized literature however, is increasing day by day and supply does not satisfy the demand. In some cases, superficial knowledge of particular fish or plant species can still lead an aquarist or prospective aquarist to losses, and even to giving up this great hobby.

Next to the characins, barbs, cichlids, livebearing tooth carps, egg laying tooth carps and catfishes, labyrinth fishes are a group which is frequently kept in the aquarium. The majority of species are colorful, and many are suited for the beginner. The purpose of this book is to examine in detail the family of labyrinth fishes and to provide all the information required to successfully keep and breed them.

For friendly encouragement and for reading the manuscript thanks are due to Professor Guenther Sterba and Mr. Helmut Stallknecht. For help with the supply of literature and verbal advice, thanks are also due to Dr. Fritz Terofel (Dept. of Zoology, Museum, Munich), Dr. Hans M. Peters (Zoo-Physiological Institute, University of Tuebingen), Dr. Herbert R. Axelrod (Neptune, New Jersey), Mr. Horst Linke (Berlin), Mr. Erhardt Roloff (Karlsruhe) and Dr. Joerg Vierke (Husum).

Dr. Jacques Gery (left) and Dr. Herbert R. Axelrod confer during collecting trip in Brazil. Dr. Axelrod is holding a photo tank.

6

Introduction to Labyrinth Fishes

Labyrinth fishes are a group of perch-like fishes, all of which have a common characteristic in having a supplementary respiratory organ.

Unlike most other fish species, which remove oxygen from the water by passing it through the gills, labyrinth fishes can obtain an additional supply from the atmosphere by using the so-called "labyrinth" organ. To do this, they must periodically swim to the water surface to exchange the gases. The gills of normally developed labyrinth fishes are degenerated to such an extent that they could not alone support the fishes' life from oxygen absorbed from the water. However, experiments have shown that, in oxygen saturated water, fish which are denied the use of their labyrinth organ would still survive.

In such cases, the number of respiratory movements per minute rose from 35-80 to 250. Furthermore, these experiments showed that in young fish denied the use of their labyrinth organs, these organs would not develop fully (only minimal capillary development in the labyrinth membrane). If these young fishes were later kept in normal conditions, then the

The labyrinth organs in the genera *Belontia* (above) and *Anabas*.

labyrinth organs would develop fully (Bader 1937). The labyrinth is a paired organ situated next to the gill cavities and consisting of folded, delicate membranes mounted on a bony frame and with a network of numerous blood capillaries. The organ functions somewhat in the manner of a lung. If a fully developed labyrinth fish in normal water conditions is denied the possibility of obtaining atmospheric oxygen, it will drown!

Introduction to Labyrinth Fishes

Appropriate experiments were performed by Day (1868), Dobson (1874), Henninger (1907) and Das (1928). The evolution of the labyrinths is dependent on the adverse nature of the habitat. Unusually high temperatures in shallow ponds etc. at certain times of the year, mean a very low oxygen content in the water.

One can easily demonstrate this with fish that require a high oxygen supply. The fish are placed in a tank of water, without plants and without a supplementary air supply, and the temperature is slowly raised to 30°C. Firstly, the fish will begin to respire more rapidly with their gills; then they will swim to the surface in order to "get some air". This is not as unlikely as it may sound as water sucked into the gills near the surface will be mixed with air.This method of obtaining oxygen is very stressful to normal fish and if they are forced to do it over a protracted period they will die.

The labyrinth fishes, during the course of evolution have developed the supplementary labyrinth respiratory organ in order to obtain oxygen directly from the atmosphere - essential for a fish that lives in that certain kind of environment. Even in water with a high oxygen content, these fishes still obtain their oxygen mainly by using the labyrinth organ; in fact, the complete oxygen requirement of the fish can be obtained through the labyrinth organ.

The frequency at which these fishes obtain air increases with rising temperatures. There are two probable explanations; firstly, warmer water has less oxygen; secondly, the rate of metabolism also increases resulting in a higher oxygen requirement. With a temperature increase of 10°C, the oxygen requirement increases by 2-3 times.

Depending on the condition of the water in which they live, particularly in relation to the oxygen content, various species of labyrinth fishes have developed an appropriate labyrinth organ. For example, the Climbing Perch, *Anabas testudineus,* which can stay out of water for fairly long periods has a relatively large highly developed labyrinth organ, while that of the Combtail, *Belontia signata,* which lives in mountain streams, is relatively small.

Labyrinth fishes from the Southeast Asian range are

mostly peaceful aquarium fish, while those native to Africa can be regarded as more or less pugnacious.

With adequate care in the aquarium, labyrinth fishes often reach a much greater age than they would in the wild, as the life support systems here are often more favorable. Some species live in the aquarium for just about 2 years, ex. Dwarf Gourami - *Colisa lalia*; others as much as 12 years, ex. Leopard Ctenopoma - *Ctenopoma acutirostre*.

10

Primitive African tribes depend heavily upon all fishes for food, regardless of their size. The labyrinth fishes are easily caught because they are not found in deep rivers, thus they are easily captured even by native children.

A knowledge of the fishes' external anatomy is very useful for recognition of the various species. The most important characteristics in species recognition include the number of fin rays, the number of scales in a lateral row and the number of scales in a diagonal row. These are given in the text on species descriptions.

In the fin formula, hard fin rays (spines) are indicated by Roman numerals, and branched, soft fin rays by Arabic numerals. The two types of rays are separated by a diagonal line. An abbreviation of the appropriate fin comes before the numerals: A = Anal Fin; C = Caudal (tail) Fin; D = Dorsal Fin; P = Pectoral Fin; V = Ventral Fin. The fin formula for *Colisa lalia* is therefore D XV-XVII/7-10: A XVII-XVIII/12-17: the dorsal has between 15 and 17 spinous rays and 7-10 soft, branched rays; the anal has 17-18 spines and 12-17 soft, branched rays.

The scales along the lateral line (lateral line row or llr) are

The meristic (countable or measurable) characteristics of a typical fish are: **A** = length of caudal peduncle; **B** = head length; **C** = snout length; **D** = total depth of body; **E** = total depth of head; **F** = body length; **G** = total length; **H** = height of caudal peduncle; **DLR** = diagonal line row or scale rows; **LLR** = lateral line row or scales along the lateral line.

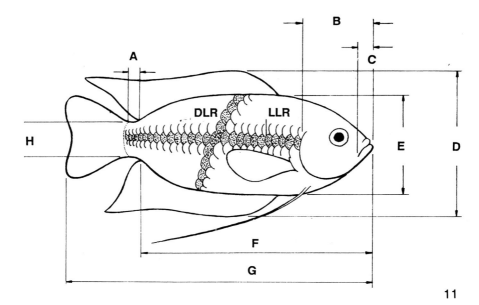

External Anatomy

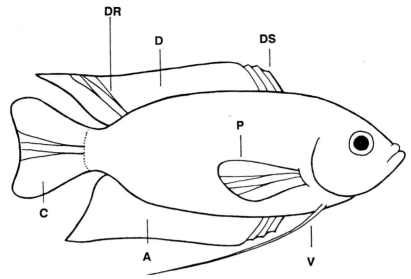

The fins of a typical labyrinth fish are: **A** = anal fin; **C** = caudal fin; **D** = dorsal fin; **P** = pectoral fin; **V** = ventral fin; **DS** = dorsal spines; **DR** = dorsal rays which are branched or soft.

The diagram above is easily understood when compared to the live Dwarf Gourami, *Colisa lalia.*

External Anatomy

counted from the upper corner of the gill opening to the base of the tail. The diagonal line (diagonal line row or dlr) scales are counted at the greatest body depth.

Other useful information given is the total length, body length, greatest body depth, tail-base height, snout length and general description of the body parts.

One should not rely too heavily on color descriptions for identification as, especially with the African labyrinth fishes, the colors can change dramatically with age and mood.

With some of the egg scattering *Ctenopoma* species, the sexes can be distinguished by barely significant features. Behind the rear edge of the eye and on the tail base the males of these species have areas of scales which have strong spines instead of the usual narrow, toothed edge (comb scales). They can best be seen through a strong lens. These special scales are particularly well developed in older males.

Betta macrostoma. The photo shows a male (with the spot in his dorsal) displaying before a female. Males in their breeding dress are *less* colored in this species. This is a very unusual characteristic. Photo by Dr. Herbert R. Axelrod.

Classification and Nomenclature

All animal and plant species on earth which have been discovered and described receive a scientific name which is unique to each species. Linnaeus was the first to use the so-called binomial system of nomenclature, in which each animal or plant species receives a name combination of genus and species. The rules for international nomenclature were first presented in 1905 at the International Zoological Congress in Paris; they are still valid to this day although modified from time to time to reflect current thinking and problems. To minimize the possibility of confusion, the genus and species, the year of first decription and the name of the author are given, in scientific publications at least. The rules of nomenclature are unfortunately somewhat obscure to the non-specialist but two of the most significant ones are given here:

If a species, for one reason or another, is given a new generic name, the name of the first author and the year of description is given in brackets. For example: *Colisa lalia* (Hamilton-Buchanan, 1822) was originally written as *Trichopodus lalia* Hamilton-Buchanan, 1822.

Family: Belontiidae

Subfamily: Belontinae
Genus: *Belontia*

Subfamily: Trichogasterinae
Genus: *Trichogaster*

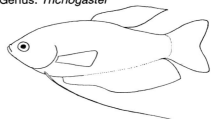

Genus: *Colisa*

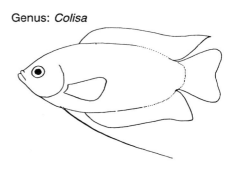

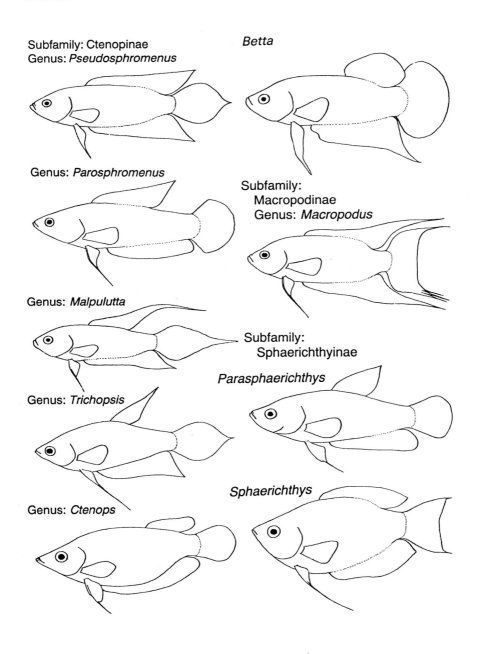

Subfamily: Ctenopinae
Genus: *Pseudosphromenus*

Betta

Genus: *Parosphromenus*

Subfamily:
Macropodinae
Genus: *Macropodus*

Genus: *Malpulutta*

Subfamily:
Sphaerichthyinae

Parasphaerichthys

Genus: *Trichopsis*

Sphaerichthys

Genus: *Ctenops*

Classification and Nomenclature

Family: Helostomidae

Subfamily: Helostominae
Genus: *Helostoma*

Genus: *Ctenopoma*

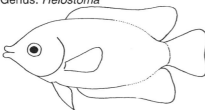

Family: Osphromenidae

Genus: *Osphronemus*

Genus: *Oshimia*

Family: Anabantidae

Genus: *Anabas*

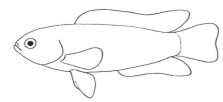

Genus: *Sandelia*

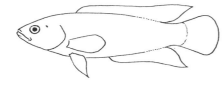

Species with minor differences warranting subspecific status, are given three names. For example: The Sumatran subspecies of the Three-spot Gourami is named *Trichogaster trichopteris sumatranus* , while the Three-spot from the South-east Asian Mainland is named *Trichogaster trichopterus trichopterus* .

Classification and Nomenclature

In this book, the following system is used:

Order Perciformes: Perch-like Fish
  Suborder Anabantoidei: Labyrinth Fishes
  Family Belontiidae
    Subfamily: Belontinae
      Genus: *Belontia*
    Subfamily: Trichogasterinae
      Genera: *Trichogaster, Colisa*
    Subfamily: Ctenopinae
      Genera: *Pseudosphromenus, Parosphromenus, Malpulutta, Trichopsis, Ctenops, Betta*
    Subfamily: Macropodinae
      Genus: *Macropodus*
    Subfamily: Sphaerichthyinae
      Genera: *Parasphaerichthys, Sphaerichthys*
  Family: Helostomidae
    Genus: *Helostoma*
  Family: Osphronemidae
    Genus: Osphronemus
  Family: Anabantidae
    Genera: *Anabas, Sandelia, Ctenopoma, Oshimia*

In view of their different breeding behavior and method of oviposition the so called "Dwarf Macropodes" have been removed from the genus *Macropodus* and placed with *Pseudosphromenus*, a revival of a genus for these species already suggested by Bleeker in 1879. The genera *Pseudosphromenus, Malpulutta, Parosphromenus, Betta, Trichopsis* and *Ctenops* have also been taken out of the subfamily Macropodinae and placed in the subfamily Ctenopinae as they all lay sinking eggs.

The above method of classification may be regarded as accurate as far as our present knowledge goes, although changes in the subfamily Ctenopinae are possible due to incomplete studies, especially in the genus *Betta*.

Evolution of the Labyrinth Fishes

In conjunction with his intensive taxonomic study of the labyrinth fishes, the American K. F. Liem (1963) also concerned himself with their evolution. Although he is due credit for his complex taxonomic work, his work on evolution, as suggested by Vierke (1975), is in need of

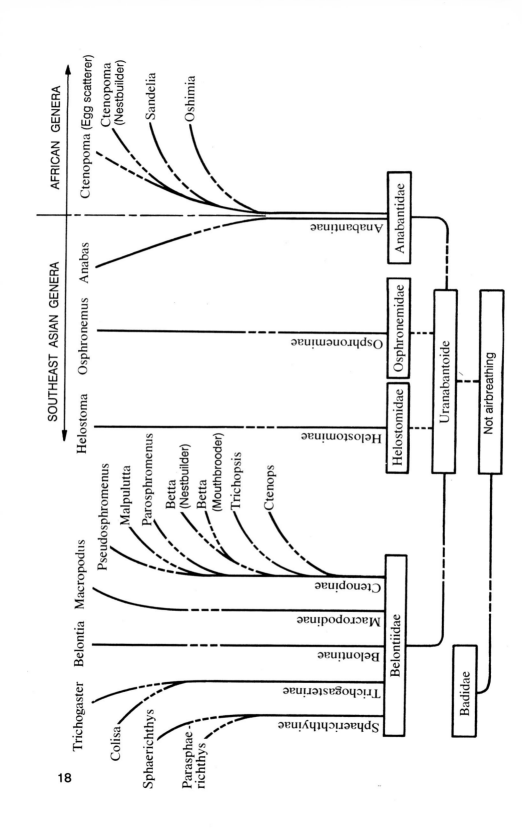

18

revision. Liem's experiments clearly showed why *Macropodus* and *Pseudosphromenus* are closely related but there are other major differences which were not considered. This is something to beware of and today these two genera most definitely do not belong in the same subfamily.

For example: the eggs of *Macropodus* float at the water surface, while those of *Pseudosphromenus* sink. In addition, there is a difference in the courtship behavior of the two genera. These are only single factors but interesting ones, if only to distinguish the differences between egg "floaters" and egg "sinkers".

It can be surmised, for instance, that reproduction through sinking eggs is more highly developed behavior than through floating ones. Proof for this theory arises from the fact that labyrinth fish that lay sinking eggs, lay fewer eggs in a breeding season than the egg floaters. This is understandable when one considers that large numbers of floating eggs must be much more difficult to protect and keep together than relatively smaller numbers of sunken eggs concealed in a

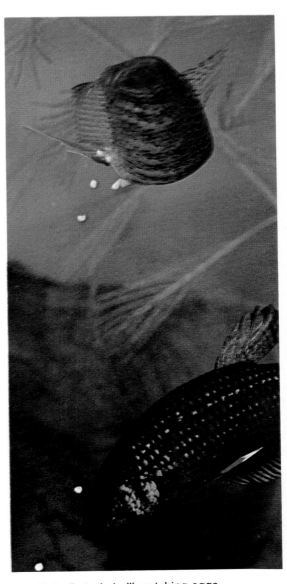

Male *Betta imbellis* catching eggs as they fall from a stunned female immediately after spawning.

submerged nook. In general, endangered species in the wild produce large numbers of eggs to continue their species survival, while common species can thrive with much lower numbers. The following numbers will give one an idea of the differences:

Floating Egg
Producers: 800-20,000 eggs
Sinking Egg Producers:
100-300 eggs.
Sinking Egg Mouthbrooders
40-80 eggs

With the mouthbrooders, a further specialization can be taken into account.

In spite of the fact that in the   genus *Betta* (fighting fish), both the sinking-egg producing nest builders and also mouthbrooders are regarded as allied; probably due to external similarities, there is no way that the genus *Sphaerichthys* (if they really exist and if mouthbrooding) and *Parasphaerichthys* can be accepted as being included with the genera *Trichogaster* and *Colisa* in one subfamily. On these grounds the family Belontiidae has here been further divided to include the subfamily Sphaerichthyinae.

It is likely that further, deep research into members of the genus *Betta* will necessarily produce two genera. Research

to date has not yet produced any firm evidence. It can be said however, that a close relationship exists between the nest building and mouthbrooding members of the genus Betta and that they possessed common ancestors.

Research into the family characteristics of the labyrinth fishes has produced the following evolutionary scheme:

a) Father family with a large number of floating-egg layers (Trichogasterinae, Anabantinae - nest-building *Ctenopoma* , Osphronemidae).

b) Father family with a small number of sinking-egg layers (Ctenopinae, with the exception of mouthbrooding *Betta*).

c) Father family with some help from the mother, at least by protection of the spawn; with a large number of floating-egg layers (Macropodinae).

d) Mother family with a small number of sinking-egg layers; mouthbrooders (Sphaerichthyinae).

e) No family protection - after spawning no further interest in eggs - with a large number of floating-egg layers (Helostomidae, Anabantinae - free-spawning *Ctenopoma*

Colisa fasciata eggs are lighter than water and they float upwards as the pair release them.

A pair of *Malpulutta kretseri* building their bubblenest in midwater under the leaf of a submersed plant.

and *Anabas*).

Although the external features of *Anabas testudineus* and *Ctenopoma nigropannosum* are very similar, their natural ranges of habitat (Southeast Asia - Africa) make the possibility of recent evolutionary relationships hardly likely. It is probable that these species have evolved completely independently of each other. As in the genus *Betta*, there are two evolutionary forms in the genus *Ctenopoma* : the free spawning and the nest building species. A division of this genus is also not to be discounted. Work on these problems is underway at the present time and final conclusions are not yet possible.

22

Natural Ranges

As far as is known, labyrinth fishes occur naturally only in eastern and southeastern Asia and western to southern Africa. By far the greatest number of genera occur in the Asian areas. The boundaries of these ranges are as follows:

— in the north; northeast China to latitude 50°N

—in the east; Korea and northeastern China to longitude 130°E

—in the west; India to longitude 70°E

—in the south; Sumatra to the equator.

There is therefore a relatively wide range of climatic factors and water conditions in the various habitats, while in the northern part of the range and in the higher altitudes of Sri Lanka (Ceylon) water temperatures can sink dramatically, those in the southern parts stay relatively high and constant. With a few exceptions, labyrinth fishes live in still to slowly flowing waters, with a high content of vegetation. Through the introduction of ditches and streams to irrigate

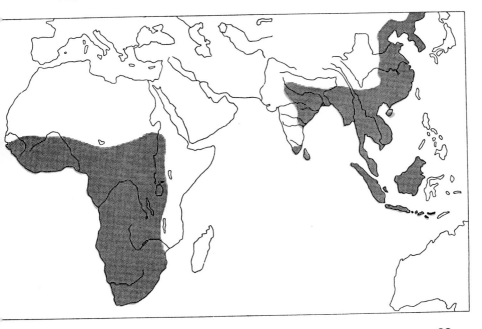

Areas of the world where labyrinth fishes are to be found.

paddy fields, especially in South-east Asia, the ranges of various species have been artificially increased. Through various circumstances (including large, cultivated breeding colonies in parts of Southeast Asia), labyrinth fishes are often found in areas where they were hitherto unknown. Reports of discoveries of labyrinth fishes in new areas should therefore be regarded with caution.

In Africa, the range of labyrinth fishes is mainly in the western and southern parts. The three known genera, *Ctenopoma, Oshimia* and *Sandelia,* occur naturally in a range extending from Senegal to South Africa. The African labyrinth fishes are mainly found in running waters, some of them in quite fast flowing streams and rivers. Some of them have even been captured under waterfalls! Many African labyrinth fishes like to conceal themselves in dark spots such as among tree roots or in cavities. The waters within the range are only sparsely vegetated with water plants *(Bolbitis*

heudelotii), though the shallows may be densely populated with *Anubias* species.

The waters within the range of the African labyrinth fishes are relatively poor in minerals with a water hardness of 6 dH and a pH value between 5 and 6.5. Water conditions vary considerably, however, due to the enormity of the range. The water temperatures are, in general, lower than those in which South-east Asian members of the suborder are found. They normally lie in the region of 22-26°C, but with seasonal variations. The majority of waters in which African labyrinth fishes are found occur in the rainforests and are only seldom directly warmed by the sun.

It must be pointed out here that the relatively high aquarium temperatures suggested in the various literature result from the fact that the water temperature is taken at the area of catching the fish—usually when it is low, and the temperature therefore relatively high.

Behavior

General Behavior

The general behavior patterns of the labyrinth fishes can be loosely divided into two groups. The first group can be classed as peaceful and will live in community with other peaceful species without any problems of aggression, while the second group can only be classed as predatory.

Those in the second group include the genera *Anabas, Belontia, Ctenopoma, Sandelia and Macropodus*. Members of these genera should therefore not be kept with other species which would be regarded as items for the menu.

While the majority of Southeast Asian labyrinth fishes are diurnal, and will show themselves, feed, court and spawn in a lit-up tank, most of the African species are nocturnal as can be assumed from their relatively large eyes. Generally, it can be said that the majority of labyrinth fish species available to the aquarist are, outside of the breeding season, relatively docile and peaceful towards other fish species.

With a few exceptions, labyrinth fishes do not damage aquatic plants. The exceptions include the Moonlight Gourami, *Trichogaster microlepis,* and the Dwarf Gourami, *Colisa lalia,* which use parts of the plants to build their nests.

Feeding Behavior

Most labyrinth fishes obtain their food mainly by snapping up small invertebrates (crustacea, insect larvae) and young fishes; in the aquarium by snapping up sinking dry food. Floating food such as dead insects and dry food in the aquarium is sucked in. In the aquarium, fish can often be observed for long periods as they sieve the water surface through the mouth and gills.

The Southeast Asian labyrinth fishes especially supplement their food with algae growing on water plants or other objects. The fish also benefit from the other tiny organisms which live in the algae.

It has occasionally been observed that some labyrinth fishes catch prey by squirting water, somewhat in the manner of the Archer Fish. Vierke (1969 - 1973) observed, filmed and reported this behavior. The fish (to date mainly *Colisa* and *Trichogaster* observed) swim to the surface and, placing themseves diagonally, observe the prey animal. Then, by sudden contractions of the mouth cavity, water drops are squirted at the prey, which is knocked off its perch and falls into the water where it is quickly snapped up by the fish.

Occasionally, capture of prey by jumping out of the water has been observed. The fish sees potential prey above the water surface and attempts to catch it. *Macropodus opercularis* is the main exponent of this method.

The red mutation of the Dwarf Gourami carrying plants to his nesting site.

Behavior

Intra-specific Aggression

Aggression and fighting are almost always related to defense of territory or spawn and the two are closely related. It is mainly the males which are actively aggressive.

The main method of winning over or retaining a territory is being able to impress the rival. This may be done in two ways, known as frontal impression and lateral impression, in which each fish attempts to show himself as stronger and bigger than his rival. With lateral impression the fish holds himself sideways to his rival, spreads all his fins to their maximum size and intensifies his color. The first fish swims past the nose of his rival in such a manner and waggles his body, in the hope that his impression will scare it away.

Frontal impression is carried out (mainly by fighting fish and macropods) by the two fishes meeting head-on, with spread fins and operculum (gill cover), which in most cases has an eye-spot. This is, in effect, a mask impression, which makes the head look much larger than it really is.

Sometimes, these impressions or occasionally without them lead further to competitions of strength in

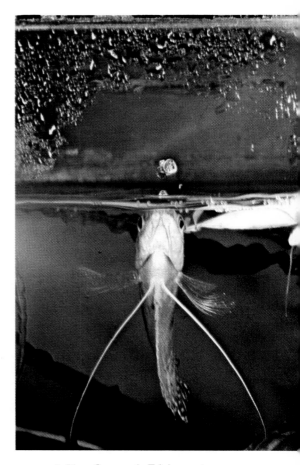

A Blue Gourami, *Trichogaster trichopterus* spitting water to capture a small fruit fly.

which the fishes attempt to push each other back by waggling the body and tail and creating water currents. This behavior will increase to ever greater intensity and, should the rival flee, will result in biting into the fins. Such behavior may be well observed in the Siamese Fighter, *Betta splendens*. For this reason, males of this species are used for

for only a short time but may repeat the action several times. To date, I have not observed any injuries from this behavior.

Fatal injuries do occur in the aquarium sometimes, especially in small aquaria, but in nature they are very rare as the defeated foe can escape in time. In the aquarium, the possibility of escape is drastically minimized.

competetive fighting in Thailand and bets are placed on the outcome.

Another method of aggression is the so called "mouth-dragging" which occurs mainly in the genera *Trichogaster* and *Anabas*. The rivals first face each other a short distance apart, then bite each other in the lips and tug backwards. They hold tightly

A male *Betta macrostoma* in a fighting pose, with his mouth wide open and all of his fins flared. The intensity of the colors is much more pronounced as the heat faded the films according to the photographer, Dr. Herbert R. Axelrod.

Behavior

During and after nest-building the male sometimes regards the female as a rival and instigates aggressive behavior. During this time, the male regards anything that even remotely resembles a fish as a rival! This behavior is particularly strong in the genera *Colisa, Betta* and *Trichogaster*.

In a too small aquarium, with no hiding places for the female, continuous biting and harrying can lead to fatalities. Great care must be taken during such times - especially if other fish are living in community.

Even the little Honey Gourami, *Colisa chuna,* will vigorously defend his brood against fish many times his own size. *Colisa lalia* for example, will immediately chase and ram any encroaching fish with his head. These butts can be so powerful as to lead to the immediate death of the attacked fish.

It is interesting to observe that Siamese Fighters, *Betta splendens,* will pause in their fighting should either rival go to the surface for air, and not take advantage of the rival's temporary helplessness. It is probable that the temporary relaxation of the spread opercula diminishes the aggression for that period.

The male *Colisa labiosa* is more colorful than the female. During spawning he often opens his mouth in the same way he would display during combat.

Reproductive Behavior

Depending on the method of brooding, labyrinth fishes can be divided into three groups: free-spawners, nest-builders and mouth-brooders.

The following text deals in detail mainly with the behavior of the nest-building species, as the majority of labyrinths fall into this category. The behavior of free-spawners and mouth-brooders is dealt with in the section on description of the species.

Apart from the singular specialties of reproductive behavior in certain species, which are discussed in the species section, all nest-building labyrinth fishes show a basic reproductive behavior common to nearly all of the species.

Reproductive behavior is first stimulated visually by recognition of the sex partners, so that the brain stimulates the release of hormones which control the functions of the sex organs. After two fishes have recognized each other as sex partners, the sex products develop in a short time (with optimum water conditions, perhaps in only a few hours). In the meantime, the male displays to the female by spreading his fins and then begins to build a bubble nest.

The method of building the bubble nest varies from genus to genus and species to species. Some build only a small nest consisting of just a few bubbles on the water surface or under the leaves of aquatic plants (some species well below the water surface). Others first prepare a sort of floating platform with pieces of vegetation before making the bubble nest beneath it (Dwarf Gourami, *Colisa lalia,* and Moonlight Gourami, *Trichogaster microlepis).* Most labyrinth fish species however build a simple bubble nest at the water surface. There are also species that build no bubble nest at all, and individual methods of nest building can vary immensely.

The nest bubbles are made by the male, who sucks in air from the water surface and spits it out as bubbles. Inside the mouth, a secretion is produced from cup-like glands, which stabilizes the bubble membranes and makes them last. As the eggs ripen in the female (this can be seen as a strong swelling in the belly), she starts trying to persuade the male to spawn. The female swims to the area,

Female *Parosphromenus deissneri* showing a crisp longitudinal pattern. Photos in this series by Dr. Walter Foersch, a leading authority on labyrinth fishes.

The eggs have fallen from the top of the cave. The male tried to care for them but quickly lost interest.

The brooding male in a typical head-down position. Note the eggs at one corner of the spawning cave.

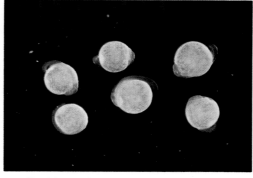

P. deissneri eggs 60 hours after being laid. The embryos can be discerned but they are not yet pigmented.

P. deissneri 12 hours after hatching.

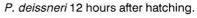

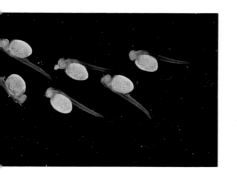

or directly to the nest, but if the nest is not yet complete she will sometimes be brutally driven away by the male. He regards the female as an enemy. This behavior is particularly common in the Dwarf Gourami, *Colisa lalia,* and the Siamese Fighter, *Betta splendens.* If the female succeeds in quickly prodding the male's body with her snout, he no longer regards her as an enemy. She is accepted as a sex partner and the preliminary pairing (no egglaying) then takes place.

With few exceptions, this form of behavior can be regarded as general. It is often observed in the aquarium, especially when separated gravid females are introduced to the breeding tank.

In the following example *(Colisa lalia)*, reproductive behavior is described as observed in a large, naturally planted aquarium:

The male has prepared his bubble nest and waits under it for a gravid female to appear. When such a female comes into his line of vision he will attempt to attract her under the nest to spawn. He swims towards her with fins spread, giving her a lateral impression, then swims back towards the nest. If the female does not follow, the process may be repeated several times. If he has a considerable distance to cover between the nest and the female, he will stop half-way and display briefly. Such behavior in the male is only successful if the female is fully gravid. A female which is not sufficiently advanced will simply swim out of his territory and she is usually not followed as another male will be trying his luck.

If the female follows the male to the nest, he stays there with spread fins and waggles his body. He awaits activity from the female. After the female has butted the male in the belly they both start to circle each other. The male bends his body and the female swims into his bodily embrace. The bodily contact of the female causes the male to cramp his body further and to grip her, turning her underside into the nest (this turning does not occur in all labyrinth fishes). The fishes stay in this position for a short time. Careful observation will reveal that the male soon begins to shiver and his body cramps further. At this moment the sperm is released by the male and shortly after, the eggs are released by the female. These travel through

Pseudosphromenus dayi male, above, building his nest of bubbles. The pair spawning in the photo below.

the sperm cloud and are fertilized. The eggs are glass clear or amber colored and float up to the water surface.

The male's bodily embrace of the female will continue for a little while. He then releases the female, which quickly swims away to a safe locality.

The male gathers together any eggs which did not end up in the nest and brings them to the nest in his mouth. More bubbles are continually added to the nest. Spawning will occur several times until the female is empty of eggs, but the male will not let her near the nest until all eggs from previous batches are safely stored in the nest. However, a snout-butt from the female will, each time, lead him to accept her as a sex partner.

After complete spawning the female must get right out of the male's sight as she will be driven off and bitten. This also goes for any other fish that gets too close to the nest.

Pseudosphromenus cupanus nest showing the eggs being supported by clear bubbles.

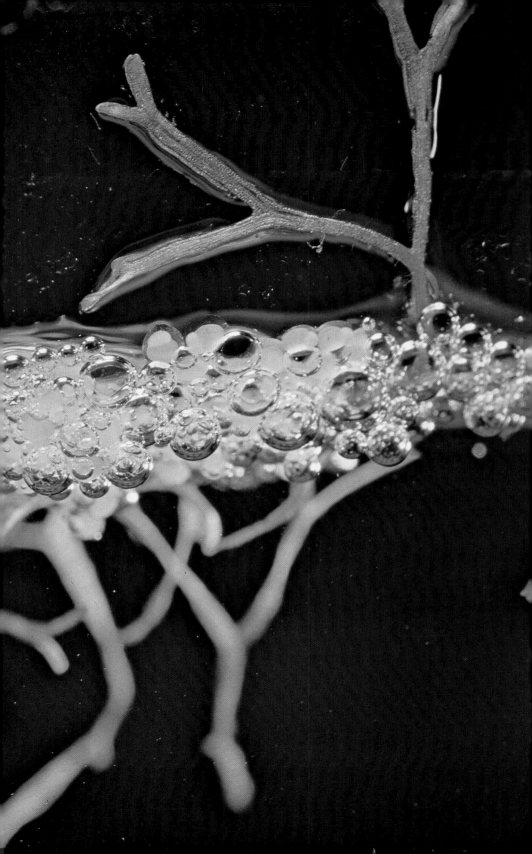

The male now busies himself in caring for the eggs. The eggs are moved and turned and new bubbles are continuously added to the nest. These are, however, not the large type bubbles with which the nest was originally built, but much smaller foam-like bubbles, prepared by forcing air through the gills. These bubbles protect the eggs on the underside of the nest.

The first larvae hatch about 24 hours after the beginning of the spawning. They possess a large yolk sac and are unable to swim. These are also looked after by the male and, should they start to sink, they are caught in the male's mouth and spat back into the nest. Three days after they hatch the young fry start to swim; the yolk sac has been absorbed and they must begin to find food. The male is no longer able to care for large numbers of free swimming fry and his brooding instinct will begin to recede; indeed he may start to eat the fry, especially if he has been poorly fed!

The fry of the Dwarf Gourami, *Colisa lalia* about 90 minutes after hatching. Photo by W. Tomey.

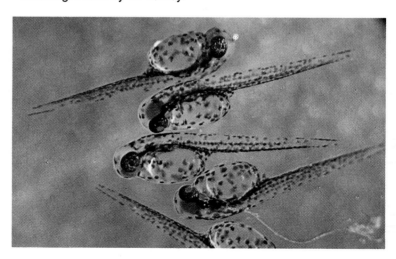

Betta smaragdina spawning. The female floats, stunned, after the male releases her from their spawning embrace. The eggs sink to the bottom as the male feverishly tries to capture them in his mouth prior to blowing them into his floating nest of bubbles.

Special Behavior

Spitting Vierke studied the spitting activities of *Colisa lalia* and *Trichogaster trichopterus* and attempted to analyze them. Spitting often occurred in the area of the nest after spawning. The water drops could be shot for up to 7cm distance and was accomplished by sudden contractions of the mouth cavity at short intervals.

I was able to observe and photograph spitting behavior in *Macropodus opercularis* as well as *Trichogaster trichopterus*. In both species this behavior occurred after spawning. In most cases the male spat out of the nest several times in a short period, onto the aquarium glass. The water drops had the effect of moving the eggs, which enabled the male to better recognize them. In the wild, the male probably spits against leaves hanging into the water for the same reason. The eggs seem to be attracted to objects hanging in the water and one can actually see them being attracted. The male spits to loosen them and move them back into the nest.

The Voice The most well-known labyrinth fishes with a voice are those in the genus *Trichopsis*. The loudest voice is possessed by the Croaking Gourami, *Trichopsis vittatus*. The croaking or growling noises can easily be heard and usually occur during territorial/sexual behavior, particularly when the fins are spread for display.

Other kinds of vocals in labyrinth fishes consist of cracking tones. Such tones have been reported from *Trichogaster leeri, T. trichopterus* and *T. pectoralis*. So far, research has not shown these types of vocalization to have any special ethological function.

Color Changing Color change is not common among labyrinth fishes. The Southeast Asian species may change color by mood. The most dramatic color changes occur in the Honey Gourami, *Colisa chuna,* the Macropods, *M. opercularis* and *M. concolor*, Java Combtail, *Belontia hasselti* and the Marbled Gourami, *Trichogaster trichopterus.*

Some of the African labyrinths change color with age. For example *Ctenopoma oxyrhynchum* and *Ctenopoma acutirostre.*

Ctenopoma ansorgii. The fish above is a young male in normal color, while the fish below is a mature male in breeding dress. Upper photo by Aaron Norman.

General Care

As already discussed, labyrinth fishes are native to waters which are relatively soft and poor in minerals when compared to other parts of the world. However, it is possible to keep these fish in hard, even very hard water, without any apparent damage to them. Most of them will even breed in such waters. One must ensure however that the water is poor in nitrates and nitrites. The following basic rules should be followed: - as large as possible aquarium - as few fish as possible - well planted - frequent water change.

Such rules appertain to all fishes. The fact that labyrinth fishes breathe atmospheric air does not mean that they cannot be poisoned via the gills, from unsuitable water. It is worth pointing out here that a normal mechanical filter will certainly make the water glass-clear in appearance but it will certainly not remove dissolved, possibly harmful chemicals from the water. One

Male Paradise Fish, *Macropodus opercularis,* building his bubblenest.

can even say that the use of a mechanical filter that is not cleaned at intervals of less than 14 days can even make the water more impure. The water is being pulled through the dirt which has already been filtered out! When such a filter is cleaned out after a long time, one can tell by the smell exactly what kind of dirt we are talking about. It should never be allowed to get so bad. The best method of controlling the purity of aquarium water is regular and frequent water changes. The larger the aquarium and the lower the number of fish, the less often is water changing necessary. The best solution would be to have a continuous

The Hockney Aquaria Filter System: (1) Filter inlet. (2) Circulation pump outlet. (3) Undergravel filter outlet. (4) Aquarium. (5) Heater. (6) Water pumps. (7) Air diffuser in contraflow compartment. (8) Filter plate. (9) Substrate. (10) Pre-filter. (11) Protein skimmer (for marine tanks usually). (12) Bypass spray bar. (13) Dry bypass filter. Wet labyrinth filter below. (14) Gravel tidy. (15) Buffering agent.

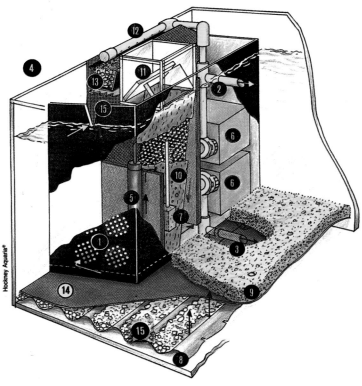

Red arrows inidcate path of dirty water from the aquarium. Yellow arrows show patch of clean, filtered water overflowing back into the aquarium.

flow of fresh water into the tank, which is practiced in some places. However, such a method is barely suitable in the home, where the possibilities of overflowing make it impracticable.

As labyrinth fishes occur in a range of sizes, aquarium size can be chosen to suit the species. For the smallest species like *Parosphromenus deissneri* and *Trichopsis pumilus* one can use an aquarium from 15l (3.3gal) upwards. For middle sized species, such as *Colisa lalia*, *C. labiosa, Trichopsis vittatus* and *Betta splendens*, an aquarium of 30l (6.6gal) plus is recommended. The large species, *Trichogaster trichopterus, T. leeri* and *Belontia signata* for example, require a tank in excess of 60l (13.3gal). The giant of the labyrinth fishes, *Osphronemus goramy,* is not recommended for the home aquarium unless one keeps juveniles for just a few months. Full grown specimens are highly regarded as food fish by the inhabitants of their native range and, as aquarium fish, they are best suited to the very big show tanks of public aquaria.

Supplementary heating of the aquarium in the home environment is barely necessary as temperatures are unlikely to fall much below 20°C and, in most cases are around 25°C. Should one require to use supplementary heating, one should ensure that a maximum of 28°C is reached. The optimal temperature for nearly all labyrinth fishes is 24-26°C.

A typical group of Kissing Gourami, *Helostoma temminckii* fry. Photo by Rudi Zukal.

They may tolerate temperatures up to 32°C for a short time but one should make it the rule preferably a few degrees lower than too high water temperatures. High temperatures shorten life, increase the likelihood of disease outbreaks, and damage the water quality (oxygen levels sink). The African labyrinth fishes in particular should not be kept above 24°C as their native waters are somewhat cooler than those from Southeast Asia. The preparation of a special aquarium for labyrinth fishes is as follows:

Substrate should consist of

The fairly plainly colored *Belontia signata* collected and photographed by Dr. Herbert R. Axelrod in Sri Lanka. It is an aggressive fish.

fine to medium gravel or shingle (2 - 5 mm grains). The back part and the sides are planted as thickly as possible with *Cryptocoryne* species. Of course, one can also use other aquatic plant species, but one must bear in mind that plants in a small aquarium will grow very quickly and will require a lot of light. Floating plants should not be used, as they grow quickly and cut out the light. For further decoration, one can use dark colored rocks and bogwood.

In introduction to the tank, the fish first of all disappear rapidly into the water plants - later they will spend more time in the open areas and will spawn there.

A single community tank is not recommended but preferably a number of species tanks as the behavior of the particular species can then be more readily observed. Once one has enough knowledge of a particular species, one can change to another so that, over a period of time, one builds up a knowledge of several species.

It is possible to keep various species of labyrinth fish together in a large tank, but one should consider the sizes and the native habitats.

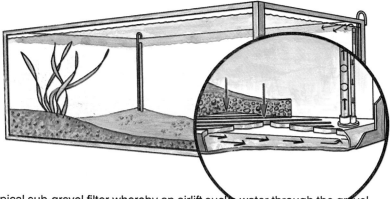

Typical sub-gravel filter whereby an airlift sucks water through the gravel into an air space under the bottom filter pad, then pushes it back to the aquarium with aeration with the aid of a pump. All these products are available at your local aquarium shop.

A typical cannister filter. The blue lines follow the path of the water which is sucked into the system from the aquarium through a coarse filter. The water is then filtered further and treated in the cannister and circulated by a pump within the cannister. It is then returned to the aquarium through the undergravel filter system which forces it through the gravel. Your local petshop can show you many kinds of filtering and aeration systems.

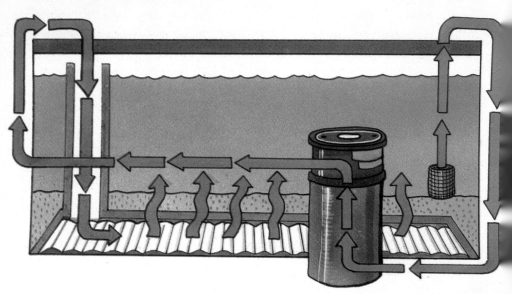

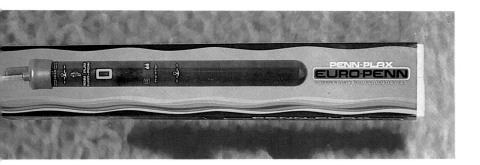

Petshops carry dependable thermostatic heaters (above) and outside paste-on thermometers as shown below.

The smallest species, such as *Parosphromenus deissneri* and *Trichopsis pumilus* are best kept on their own.

The feeding of labyrinth fishes is, with a few exceptions, relatively problem free. *Daphnia, Cyclops, Tubifex,* Enchytrae, mosquito larvae, *Drosophila* and even dry food can be given. Live food should always have priority. One should be careful not to overfeed; a daily feeding of a little food (what can be eaten in 5 minutes) is adequate. In large, well-planted aquaria, labyrinth fishes will tolerate starve-days.

Pseudosphromenus dayi male building a bubblenest under a leaf.

It is no exaggeration to say that one can go on holiday for 14 days and leave the fish to their own devices. Beware however, not to leave any supplementary heating on during the summer months. One never knows how hot it will get during one's absence and, as already pointed out, a few degrees cooler is infinitely better than cooking your fish.

Predatory species should, at least occasionally, be given young or small fish as food to supplement their diet. This applies especially to the larger *Ctenopoma, Sandelia, Anabas* and *Belontia* species.

In general, labyrinth fishes can be described as easy to care for, even taking into consideration the extreme differences in water quality described from the various collection areas.

Breeding Labyrinth Fishes

The conditions described for general care already provide a suitable environment for the successful breeding of the majority of species. An increase in temperature, which is often recommended in the literature as an aid to breeding, is not necessary. Experience has shown that most labyrinth fish, with correct conditions and care will breed just as well at a water temperature of 24°C as at 28°C. A temperature rise cannot be discounted as a stimulus to breeding but in most cases it is not neccessary.

Should one want one's labyrinth fishes to breed on command, it is necessary to keep the sexes separate prior to introducing them together in a breeding tank. One should have fresh water in the breeding tank. As many labyrinth fishes build a bubble nest or at least their spawn floats to the surface, it is not difficult to see when they have spawned. In many species the

Top: Male Paradise Fish, *Macropodus opercularis,* building his bubblenest. Below: The pair in nuptual embrace under the nest.

male looks after the brood. It is recommended that females are removed from the tank once the male has started brooding.

The male should be removed from the tank shortly before the fry become free swimming (usually three days after the spawning). One can also move the whole bubble nest to another tank just as one would the spawn of the non-brooding species, in order to have them immediately in a rearing tank. The rearing tank requires no furnishings other than a fine aerator.

Most labyrinth fish fry hatch from the eggs about 24 hours after spawning. Like most labyrinth fish eggs, the fry are covered with tiny oil bubbles which give them their buoyancy. The little bubbles are arranged along the flanks, enabling the fry to stay at the water surface. These oil bubbles are usually absorbed within the first 14 days. The relatively large yolk sac, from which the fry gains its nutrients for the first three days, is also slowly absorbed.

Top: The female Paradise Fish approaches the male for further spawning. Below: Their successful embrace produces lots of eggs.

Breeding Labyrinth Fishes

In this time, the swim bladder develops and, in most cases, the fry are able to swim freely within three days. Now is the time to start feeding them. The best food is rotifers *(Rotatoria)*. One can also use tiny *Cyclops* nauplii, but there is a danger here that these will grow too quickly and become a hazard to the fry. The young of labyrinth fishes require a great deal of food in the early days and the water should be literally alive with rotifers, so that the fry can easily find them.

Nauplii should not be given in these first few days, but as the fry grow, perhaps after a week, *Cyclops* nauplii or *Artemia* can be given. It is a good idea to include some water snails (small apple snails) in the rearing tank. These will eat up the dead food particles and help prevent fouling of the water, as well as keeping the glass clean to a certain extent. Water should be changed (preferably two thirds) every other day. The water should be siphoned out through a

Top: Spawning of the Paradise fish continues for quite a while. Below: Sometimes only a few eggs are released. . sometimes none!

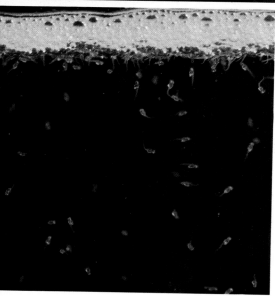

small funnel over which nylon gauze has been stretched. The replacement water should be brought up to the correct temperature and slowly added through a 4mm air tube. When the fry have grown larger, a funnel is no longer required and the water can be simply siphoned out with an air tube with a glass end on it. The mulm can then be removed from the bottom of the tank.

Next to adequate food, regular water changing in the rearing tank is essential for quick and healthy growth of the fry.

At two weeks old, the young fish will be able to eat small *Cyclops*. With rational rearing, most labyrinth fish are large enough to be sold in 8-10 weeks.

Naturally, one can also use commercially produced fry food, milk powder and self-cultured *Paramecium* to rear the fry, but results are not usually as good as when one uses freshly caught live-food.

Top: The pair embrace very close to the nest, but rarely break it. Below: In about 24 hours the fry hatch and try to swim back into the nest as they fall out.

Mutations, Varieties and Hybrids

The numbers of fish species in the wild are so great, that one wonders whether the creation of further varieties, mutations and hybrids in the aquarium is necessary. This question often leads aquarists to heated discussion. A conclusion to this discussion is not likely to materialize in the near future as everyone has his own firm and different opinions on the subject.

In nature, the environmental conditions will decide whether a new form (produced by mutation or perhaps by hybridization) can exist with its new characteristics. Only those forms (including shape, color, and locomotion) which can adapt to the environmental conditions will survive. Therefore, albinos, xanthorous or long-finned forms are rarely found in the wild as their coloring or helplessness in movement quickly makes them the victims of predators.

In scientific research, the crossing of species in the aquarium is often essential. Questions may be answered about the relationships of species and their classification and interspecific crosses provide some good information.

Aquarists have also produced some interesting results in producing various

Many slight color varieties of Paradise Fish exist. Most are faded when compared to wild fishes. Imports of new "blood" are non-existent because the fish breed so easily and prolifically.

Mutations, Varieties and Hybrids

hybrids and varieties (discus, angelfish, guppies, swordtails and platys for example).

Selective breeding has also produced some remarkable forms; often through many generations (goldfish, lyretails, ornamental (koi) carp for example). With labyrinth fishes, many varieties, hybrids and mutations have also been produced in the aquarium and some of these are now established.

Mutations

Mutations are inherited changes which are not necessarily a result of interspecific crossings. There are two types, spontaneous mutations which are usually barely discernible, and artificial mutations, induced by such factors as X-rays, colchicine, acenapthene, extreme temperatures, etc.

Mutations arise suddenly and can take many different forms. Shape, color, size, metabolism and behavior can change. Occasionally, the changes can be so great that the product is noticeably different from the normal form, but usually the changes are so insignificant that they are barely observed.

A German strain of Paradise Fish, *Macropodus opercularis*. Photo by Burkhard Kahl.

Mutations, Varieties and Hybrids

An albino strain of *Macropodus opercularis* from Czechoslovakia. Photo by Jaroslav Elias.

In the aquarium, various mutations of labyrinth fishes have been produced and nurtured. It is possible that these mutations have also appeared in the wild (albinism, xanthorism), but they would not adapt to the environment and would soon be lost. The labyrinth fish mutations known to date are as follows:

Macropodus opercularis
An albino form
A male with three scalloped fin

Anabas testudineus
Xanthorous form

Helostoma temmincki
Xanthorous form

Trichogaster trichopterus
Golden Gourami
Silver Gourami

Betta splendens
Xanthorous form
Black form

Varieties

By selection of the parents, varieties can be produced which are improved from generation to generation as the desired characteristics increase with the numbers produced. By pairing the fishes which show the most desirable characteristics, these will be further strengthened in the offspring. As an example, a *Colisa lalia* male with intensive coloration and the correct (in human opinion) body stripes would be used for breeding. This would not produce anything new, but would ensure the chances of some of the male's good points being passed on to the next generation. As another example: macropods have been selectively bred to produce ever longer and more beautiful finnage.

Great excitement is still shown at the Fighting Fish shows. The Siamese Fighter is still very popular and there are many varieties. In Thailand, these fish are specially bred for their prowess in combat (the fighters are selectively bred) whereas aquarists breed them more for color and form (especially with regard to the finnage). The following forms are popular: Red with normal, long finnage; Blue with normal, long finnage; Red, blue, normal, opaline, brown and black with veil finnage.

Hybrids

Individuals of a species breed readily together, even races and subspecies at the borders

Right: A pair of the Czech strain of albino Paradise Fish, *Macropodus opercularis,* spawning. Photo by Jaroslav Elias.

A hybrid probably between *Macropodus opercularis* and *M. concolor.* Photo by Arend van den Nieuwenhuizen.

Mutations, Varieties and Hybrids

of their ranges, thus producing new gene combinations and a diversity of characteristics *(Trichogaster trichopteris)*. Individuals of different species can occasionally, in certain circumstances (sex drive), produce offspring but these are rarely fertile. The species is therefore a genetical unit.

Two male Siamese Fighting Fish, *Betta splendens*. The fish below has a split tail (a fixed strain) with a very thick, deep caudal peduncle. His dorsal fin begins far forward almost even with the origin of his anal fin. The male on the facing page is much more slender. His caudal peduncle is narrow, his body elongated and his dorsal insertion set far back beginning over the middle of his anal. Photo by A. Roth and Michael Gilroy (facing page).

Mutations, Varieties and Hybrids

Crosses which we are about to discuss often produce sterile hybrids, but are influenced by the closeness of the relationship of the species used. However, as far as labyrinth fishes go, we are still in the very early stages of hybrid producing. Crosses have been both accidental and intended (in order to prove or disprove the possibility). For successful results a knowledge of the rules of Mendelism is required.

If two pure races or species are crossed together, the offspring of the first filial generation (F1) are all similar. They can either take a mixture of characteristics from both parents or take those from the dominant parent while those from the recessive parent are suppressed.

A very attractive hybrid is produced with *Macropodus opercularis* × *M. concolor*. In this case, the offspring take characteristics from both

This nice yellow double-tail female won Best-in-Show for Dennis Sommers. The white in her anal pore indicates she is ready for spawning. Photo by Al Liebetrau.

parents.

A hybrid which does not acquire the beauty of either parent is *Colisa lalia* × *C. labiosa*. The hybrids all turned out to be phenotypical males and were probably sterile (Vierke 1972).

Vierke also produced hybrids from *Trichopsis vittatus* and *T. schalleri* (1975). The offspring are not as attractive as either parent but they are fertile and can produce further offspring. This caused Vierke to doubt that *T. schalleri* is a true species. I have succeeded in producing offspring from a pairing of *T. schalleri* with *T. pumilus*. The hybrids are also fertile.

In Moscow, I was shown hybrids resulting from *T. leeri* × *T. trichopterus;* unfortunately these were still juvenile, so that I was unable to see the end result.

Crossings of *Betta splendens* with *Pseudosphromenus dayi* have occurred many times, but the fry have not lived for more than 24 hours after hatching (Richter 1972).

Especially beautiful results have resulted from crossing the various *Betta* varieties. By crossing the veilfin with the wild form, some really remarkable color varieties have been produced. A crossing of *B. imbellis* × *B. splendens* (veilfin) has produced beautifully colored hybrids which are also fertile.

60

Diseases of Labyrinth Fishes

The most well-known disease of labyrinth fishes is the so called "Colisa Disease" which is caused by the parasite *Oodinium pillularis,* a flagellate. Full grown, the parasite does not resemble a flagellate but sits on the skin as a spherical to pear-shaped object. The ripe parasite falls from the fish and encapsulates itself in the substrate. Here, the parasite divides until a swarm of flagellates appear; each one of these requires a fish host to complete its life-cycle.

Oodinium pillularis does not only attack *Colisa lalia* and other labyrinth fishes but nearly all fish species. The diseased fish show a velvet-like, white to golden-yellow bloom on the scales; sometimes compared with a sprinkling of flour. The gills and the intestines are also infested. The infected fish will make scratching motions against objects in the water as if attempting to relieve the irritation and those fish with badly infested gills will show difficulty in respiring. In bad infestations the fish will slowly die. However a cure is usually successful. The fish are removed to a tank containing tapwater and 2 dessert spoons of cooking salt per 10 litres. After a few days, the fish should be fully cured. The tank which contained the infected fish should be left for a few days without fish so that the flagellates do not find a host and will die off.

Another flagellate disease is *Costia* which also attaches itself to the skin and gills. This is also pear-like in shape and infected fish swim slowly and scratch themselves against objects. *Costia* usually affects weak or stressed fish. Infected fish are removed to another tank (without furnishings other than an aerator) where the temperature is raised to 32°C. After 4-6 hours the fish are removed to a further tank of water containing Trypaflavine and the temperature is maintained for a few days at 28-30°C. During the treatment, it is best to feed the fish just with Enchytrae.

Now and again, fish can be weakened against viral attacks by one sided feeding, especially by giving them a large proportion of Enchytrae in their diet. In such cases, the food can introduce the infectious, dropsical bacterial disease, *Pseudomonas punctata* into the tank. Symptoms include a swelling up of the body, usually with scales standing out.

The life cycle of "Colisa disease", *Oodinium pillularis* as it attacks a male Siamese Fighting Fish. Drawn by John Quinn.

Treatment is difficult and it is best to destroy infected fish, move other fish to another tank and to sterilize the infected tank and its contents.

A similar course should be taken if fish tuberculosis, *Mycobacterium piscium*, occurs. It is difficult to diagnose this disease from symptoms alone as these are so variable, but it may be diagnosed by special examination. Fish suffering from the disease lose their appetites, lose weight (becoming hollow-bellied), develop goggle-eyes and swollen or flat blemishes.

Contributory causes to an outbreak of such diseases include keeping fish at sub-optimum conditions. A few years ago, the disease was common in *Ctenopoma fasciolatum* and *Colisa lalia* but it was cured by lowering the temperature in the aquarium to a level similar to that of the native habitat.

Family Belontiidae

Subfamily Belontinae.

Genus *Belontia Myers, 1923. The name is taken from the local name Belontja in Palembang, used for B. hasselti.* Number of Species: 2. Size: 150-200 mm Shape: Elongate. Fin Formation: Ventrals (1/5), 16-20 hard and 9-13 soft dorsal rays, 13-17 hard and 10-13 soft anal rays.

Belontia hasselti

Belontia hasselti (Cuvier, 1831). Java Combtail *hasselti* - from van Hasselt. Local Name: Belontjain, Palembang. Other Names in the Literature: *Polycanthus hasselti* Cuvier, 1831; *P. kuhlii* Bleeker, 1845; *P. einthovenii* Bleeker, 1851; *P. helfrichtii* Bleeker, 1855; *P. hasselti* var. *einthoveni* Vaillant, 1893. First Description: Cuvier and Valenciennes (1831): *Histoire naturelle des poissons,* 7. Natural Range: Java in the area of Jakarta, Kalimantan (Borneo), Sumatra, Singapore, Malayan Peninsula. Ecology: Found in slow moving, clear waters. Total Length: Male 195mm, female 175mm. Sex Recognition: Male: slimmer body, unpaired fins larger and longer flowing, color pattern more prominent than in female; Female: Stockier body, unpaired fins smaller and shorter flowing, lighter color, less obvious pattern than in male. Description: Fins: D XVI-XX/10-13, A XV-XVII/11-13, P 11-13, V I/5, C 1-16-1. Scales: llr 30-32, dlr 5-6-1-12-15. Captive Care: In view of its large size *B. hasselti* is not an aquarium fish in the true sense. It should only be kept in tanks larger than 100 l capacity. For optimal conditions a well planted substrate with adequate hiding places and regular water changing is recommended. The water may be soft or hard but a pH of 7 and a temperature of 20-26°C is recommended.

Other fish, providing they are not less than 5cm in length can be safely kept in community. Feed with a variety of livefoods and some dry food. Earthworms, mosquito larvae, water beetle larvae, and small fish such as guppies are eaten greedily, especially after lights out.

A specialty of this species is its regular color changing in

which dark color bands appear for various reasons; for example, at rest, in excitement, in stress situations and after shock. In stress situations, the male develops deep black spots in the lines of his network pattern.

To breed this species it is best to keep them in single pairs in a large aquarium. When ready to spawn, the fishes show their dark coloration and pattern. The male swims around the female and makes waggling movements with his body; then places himself at right angles to her. The waggling motions continue. Only a suggestion of a bubble nest is built prior to spawning this usually in the corner of the tank or under floating plants. The female is then taken into a bodily embrace by the male and her underside is turned towards the water surface. The eggs are light-yellow in color and are about 1.5mm in diameter. They float to the surface. Only after completion of the spawning are the eggs gathered together by the male and taken to the bubble nest.

At 25°C, the fry will hatch in 2 days and are further guarded by the male until they swim freely after about 3 days.

Nauplii and microworms are recommended for first food. Numbers of fry: 500-700. The female takes on a light color during and after spawning and she is not allowed near the nest once the eggs are laid. She must hide or she will be attacked by the male. Juvenile fish show a dark eye-spot on the upper rear part of the body.

Special Behavior: When feeding, one can sometimes hear a staccato, cracking noise. Acclimatized fish have their own sleeping places and sometimes actually lay on their sides. One could imagine, in the first instance, that the fish is dead! This happens even during the daytime.

Belontia signata

Belontia signata (Guenther, 1861). Ceylon Combtail. *signata* (Lat.)—marked. Local Names: Pulutta, Kola modeya (Sinhalese). Other Names in the Literature: *Polycanthus signatus* Guenther, 1861. First Description: Guenther (1861): *Catalogue of the fishes in the collection of the British Museum, 3 (Polycanthus signatus).* Natural Range: Sri Lanka (Ceylon) - North-West Province: Butuluoya, Chilaw,

64

Kurunegala; West Province: Attidiya, Barueliya, Moratuwa, Tebuwana, Yakwala; Sabaragamuwa Province: Balainna, Nambapana, Warakapola. Ecology: According to Deraniyagala this species lives in colonies near to sunken tree trunks or in root systems and water plants; in mountain streams, lowland rivers, and ponds. According to Jonklaas, the fish are found in most parts of Sri Lanka in clear rivers. In exceptional circumstances they are found in lakes which completely dry out in the dry season.

Together with Jonklaas and Geisler, Bader collected *B. signata, Barbus nigrofasciatus, Noemacheilus striatus, Rasbora vaterifloris*, catfishes and loaches, in the Andonawa River, altitude 300m, near to Ratnapura. Here, the river was heavily shaded by forest trees on both sides and the banks thickly grown with *Lagenandra ovata*. The river itself was free of aquatic vegetation. The fishes mainly stayed near to the banks under overhanging vegetation. The water qualities (after Geisler) were dH O.65, ph 6.68 (measured electrically), iron content 0.13mg/l, water temperature 28.1°C. Total Length: Male about 147mm, female about 135mm. Sex Determination: It is difficult to immediately distinguish the sexes. However, it is quite easy with full grown and well fed specimens. The males are slimmer than the females and the fins are more elongated. After feeding and prior to spawning, females show a swollen belly.

Description: Fins: D XVI-XVII/9-10, A XIII-XVI/10-12, P 11-13, V I/5, C 15-1. Scales: llr 29-30, dlr 3-3½-1-9. Captive Care: Because of its large size, this species should only be kept in a large tank and preferably only a small number of specimens. A single pair per tank is best. In spite of the size, this species is so attractive as to warrant keeping. Aquarium preparation as for *B. hasselti*. Fighting will occur if the tank is too small. Like *B. hasselti, B. signata* also makes sleeping places. Breeding is possible in the community tank. The *B.*

signata male shows strong territorial behavior in the breeding season however and all other fishes are driven out of his territory. The male builds a suggestion of a bubble nest under a floating leaf and after a few trial pairings, spawning occurs. The female is taken into a bodily embrace by the male and her underside is held towards the water surface. About 40 eggs are laid at a time and these are collected together by the male and placed in the bubble nest. After each spawning act the female is driven away and she will hide until the male requires her for the next spawning. After completion of spawning, the male enlarges the nest and places the eggs in one or two spots in it. The male drives all other fish away from the nest area, but the female is allowed to stay near the nest, where she also guards it from a distance.

Altogether, about 500 eggs may be laid by large specimens, like those of *B. hasselti*, these are relatively large with a diameter of about 1.2mm and clear yellow in color. The fry hatch in about 30 hours and swim freely within 3 days. They are then relatively large at 6mm. The fry

can be reared on nauplii. The young are kept in a loose group and guarded by both parents. The juveniles show a dark eye-spot at the upper, rear half of the body; this gradually disappears as the fish mature. Special Behavior: When displaying, the fish show dark, continuous, transverse bands and a dark patch in the rear of the dorsal fin. Miscellaneous: Three geographical races of *B. signata* have been described by Benl and Terofal (1975): 1. A high-backed, stocky form in which the total body length is at the most, three times the height. There is no marking on the pectoral. There is no blue on the body. 2. A slender type, which is more than three times longer than its body height (not including the fins). Very colorful, showing metallic blue in the lower half of the body. There is usually a turquoise-blue patch on the pectoral. Juveniles are plainly colored. 3. An intermediate form of 1 and 2.

Top, left: Male *Belontia hasselti* in normal coloration. Top, right: The same fish in breeding color. Below: A male *Belontia signata*.

67

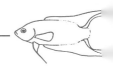

Subfamily Macropodinae
Genus *Macropodus*
Lacepede, 1802. makros (Gr.)-
large, long; pous, podus - foot.
Number of Species: 3. Size:
60-120mm. Fin Formation:
short ventrals (I/5), 12-18 hard
and 5-9 soft dorsal rays, 17-20
hard and 9-15 soft anal rays.
The posterior dorsal and anal
rays run out to a point.

Macropodus chinensis

Macropodus chinensis
(Bloch, 1790). Round-tailed
Paradise Fish. *chinensis* -
after the range of distribution.
Other Names in the Literature:
Chaetodon chinensis Bloch,
1790 *Polycanthus chinensis*
Cuvier and Valenciennes,
1831; *P. paludosus*
Richardson, 1842;
Macropodus opercularis
Regan, 1909; *M. ctenopsoides*
Brind, 1915; *M. chinensis*
Myers, 1925.
First Description: Bloch
(1790): *Naturgeschichte der
auslaendischen Fische,* Tafel
CCXVIII, I *(Chaetodon
chinensis).* Natural Range:
Southern China and Korea.
Ecology: All kinds of waters
but those densely vegetated
with aquatic plants. Total
Length: 60mm. Sex
Determination: Male more
vividly patterned and colored,
female a little smaller.
Description: Fins: D XIV-
XVIII/5-8, A XVIII-XX/9-12.
Scales: llr 28-30; dlr 14.
Captive Care: This species has
not been seen in the general
aquarium trade for some
years. From its natural range it
would seem to require similar
conditions to the two following
species, but a little cooler.
Miscellaneous: Schwier (1939)
reported a cross between *M.
opercularis* and *M. chinensis;*
the male hybrids were sterile
but the females were fertile.

Macropodus concolor

Macropodus concolor Ahl,
1937. Black Paradise Fish.
concolor (Lat.)—uniformly
colored. Other Names in the
Literature: *M. opercularis
concolor* Ahl, 1937
First Description: Ahl (1937):
Neue Suesswasserfische aus
dem indischen und
malaiischen Gebiet. *Zool.
Anzeiger,* S. 117-118. Natural
Range: Unknown. Total
Length: Male about 120mm,
female about 80mm. Sex

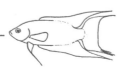

Female *Betta fasciata*. Photo by Ed Taylor.

Determination: The male has longer fin pennants and a larger area of finnage. The female has a lighter colored belly, especially when gravid. Description: Fins: D XII/9, A XVIII/14, V I/5, C13. General Care: This species is best kept in a large aquarium (greater than 50l capacity). As they can be aggressive against other fish, especially when rearing a brood, thick planting is recommended so that plenty of refuges are available. The foreground is left open or only planted with short plants. The male builds a large bubble

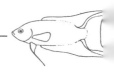

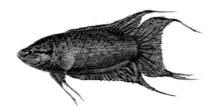

nest with relatively large bubbles. During the breeding period, the male takes on a dark color, which has given the name Black Paradise Fish. Exactly the opposite occurs with the female and she takes on a very light coloration. After spawning, she will again darken. After spawning, the male becomes extremely aggressive and will even attack a finger placed near to the bubble nest. Misc: This species is sometimes regarded as a subspecies of *M. opercularis* and hybrids can be produced from the two forms. Myers considers *M. opercularis concolor* Ahl, 1937, as a southern subspecies of *M. opercularis.*

Macropodus opercularis

Macropodus opercularis (Linnaeus, 1758). Paradise Fish. *operculum* (Lat.)—gill cover. Other Names in the Literature: *Labrus opercularis*

Linnaeus, 1758; *L. operculatus* Gmelin, 1788; *Macropodus viridi-auratus* Lacepede, 1802; *Platypodus furca* Lacepede, 1804; *Macropodus ocellatus* Cantor, 1842; *Macropodus venustus* Cuvier and Valenciennes, 1846; *Polyacanthus opercularis* Richardson, 1842; *P. paludosus* Richardson, 1842; *Macropodus viridi-auratus* Guenther, 1861; *Polyacanthus viridi-auratus* Weis, 1878; *P. opercularis* var. *viridiauratus* Koehler; *Macropodus opercularis* Regan, 1909; *Polyacanthus operculatus* Oshima, 1919; *Macropodus filamentoşus* Oshima; *M. opercularis* var. *viridi-auratus* Bade 1923.

First Description: Linnaeus (1758): *Systema Naturae;* 10th edition, p. 283. Natural Range: China, Korea, Viet Nam and Taiwan. Ecology: Shallow waters of all kinds. Total Length: Males to 110mm,

Top, left: Paradise Fish, *Macropodus opercularis*. Top, right: Albino form of *Macropodus opercularis*. Bottom, left: Cross between *M. opercularis* and *concolor*. Bottom, right: *M. concolor.*

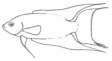

females about 80mm. Sex Determination: Males have a more intense coloration and larger fins. Females are smaller, more sombrely colored and have shorter fins. Description: Fins: D XIII-XVII/6-8, A XVII-XX/11-15, P 11, V I/5. Scales: llr 28-31. Captive Care: Its wonderful colors make the Paradise Fish a very popular aquarium subject. Thriving at temperatures of 15-20°C it is easy to keep. Temperatures over 24°C should however be avoided. Water hardness is not important. One should beware however, of the belligerence of this species towards other fish, especially during the breeding time. It should be kept in an aquarium with a minimum capacity of 50l, preferably in single pairs, but breeding is possible in the community tank. The male builds a thin bubble nest with large bubbles. At spawning time, the female can also become aggressive towards other fishes in the tank and she will help collect the eggs together in the nest and to guard the brood. It has been observed that if the male is removed, the female will continue to guard the nest and brood on her own for up to 8 days. Juveniles of this species, in contrast to those of other labyrinth species, are guarded for quite a long period. Given a special sign, the fry will swim directly to the parents. Special Behavior: After spawning, spitting behavior may be commonly observed with this species.

Subfamily Ctenopinae Genus *Pseudosphromenus* Bleeker, 1879. Number of Species: 3 Size: 65-70mm. Shape: Elongate. Fin Formation: short ventrals (I/5), 13-17 hard and 5-7 soft dorsal rays, 16-21 hard and 9-12 soft anal rays. The dorsal, anal and caudal run into points.

Pseudosphromenus cupanus

Pseudosphromenus cupanus (Cuvier and Valenciennes, 1831). Spike-tailed Paradise Fish. *cupanus* - taken from d'Arian-Coupang (river in Pondichery). Other Names in the Literature: *Polyacanthus cupanus* Cuvier and Valenciennes, 1831; *Pseudosphromenus cupanus* Bleeker, 1879; *Macropodus cupanus* Regan, 1909. First Description: Cuvier and Valenciennes (1831): *Histoire naturelle des poissons, 7, p. 357.* Natural Range: Southern India and Sri Lanka. Ecology: Small, coastal rivers; mostly highly vegetated. Total Length: about 65mm. Sex

Determination: Males more colorful, especially more red in the fins. Female becomes very dark shortly before spawning. Description: Fins: D XIV-XVII/5-7, A XVI-XIX/9-11, P 11-12, V I/5. Scales: llr 29-32. Captive Care: *P. cupanus* is regularly imported and reports on care and breeding are numerous. A 30l tank is adequate for one or two pairs. Plant thickly at the rear with feathery plants and a single, free standing, broad-leafed plant in the foreground. This way, one can easily observe the spawning, which will (usually) take place under one of the broad leaves. Should such a leaf not be available, the nest will simply be made at the water surface. As he builds his bubble nest, the male takes on a beautiful coloration, while the female, at this time , becomes nearly black. During spawning, the female will be sometimes turned to an extent that her head is pointing vertically downwards. After releasing the spawning embrace, the male may have eggs resting on his anal fins. These soon fall off and are gathered up by both sexes which then swim to the bubble nest. Should the female start storing the eggs in the nest first, she may continue to do so; but if the

male starts first, the female is no longer allowed to place her snout in the nest. In the latter case, the female will spit the eggs towards the nest from a distance and the male will then collect them and store them. The eggs are whitish and heavier than water and are first made buoyant after being turned around in the parents' mouths and covered with tiny bubbles. After the eggs have all been stored in the nest the female is driven off. About 300 eggs are produced in an hour. It has been frequently observed that,

a few hours after spawning, a male will build a new bubble nest, to which the eggs are then transferred. Reasons for this are unknown. The fry hatch in about 30 hours and, after 3 days they become free swimming. The fry may be reared on infusoria. For best results, the fry should be moved to a separate container one day before they become free swimming. Special Behavior: Females will care for the brood as well as the males if the latter are removed. Misc:

This is a spawning series of *Pseudosphromenus cupanus*. The
sequence runs along the top row, from left to right, then the bottom row
from left to right. The male builds a nest under a leaf. The female joins

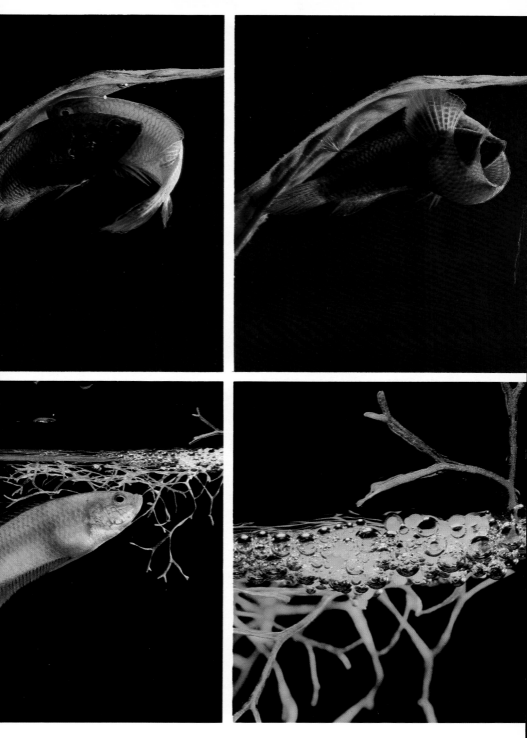

him. The male folds his body. They embrace. The embrace produces falling eggs. The male catches them. The male blows them into his nest. The eggs float on top of the nest.

This species tolerates relatively low temperatures and the water temperature can sink below 18°C without any harm to them.

Pseudosphromenus dayi

Pseudosphromenus dayi(Koehler, 1909). Red Spike-tailed Paradise Fish. *dayi* - after Francis Day (1829-89). Other Names in the Literature: *Polyacanthus cupanus* var. Day, 1878; *P. cupanus* var. *dayi* Koehler, 1909; *Parosphromenus deissneri* Juerss, 1912; *Macropodus cupanus* var. Wolterstorff, 1912; *M. cupanus* var. *dayi* Steche, 1914; *M. c. dayi* Myers, 1925; *Pseudosphromenus cupanus dayi* Vierke, 1975. First Description: Koehler (1909): *Blaetter,* p. 331 *(Polyacanthus cupanus* var. *dayi).* Natural Range: Southern Viet Nam. Ecology: In vegetated flowing waters. Total Length: 70mm. Sex Determination: Only possible by fully grown individuals. Males are slimmer; often with red throat. Fin pennants longer in male. Females plumper and lighter colored in the belly region. Description: Fins: D XIII-XVII/5-7, A XVI-XXI/10-12. Scales: llr 27-30. Captive Care: See *P. cupanus*; single pairs

are recommended. Special Behavior: Several males in a tank will become territorially aggressive, resulting in damage to fins. Misc: Although sometimes regarded as a subspecies of *P. cupanus,* it is more likely that this is a species in its own right.

Parosphromenus parvulus

Parasphromenus parvulus Vierke, 1979. *parvulus* (Lat.) – very small First Description: Vierke (1979): Ein neuer Labyrinthfisch von Borneo - *Parasphromenus parvulus* nov. spec. *Das Aquarium,* pp. 247-250. Natural Range: Mentaya river system, about 250km north west of Banjarmasin, Kalimantan (south Borneo). Ecology: Narrow, slow moving jungle stream with clear, but cola-colored water. Water temperature about 24°C (March 1978 around 8 a.m.),

A pair of *Pseudosphromenus dayi*.

pH under 4.8. Banks with large-leaved Araceae and grass. Total Length: 27mm. Sex Determination: Male intensively colored. Female yellowish brown; fins almost transparent. Description: Fins: D X-XI/7, A VIII-IX/10-11, V I/5, C 12. Scales: llr 26-27 (1 or 2 on the tail base). Captive Care: Although found in very soft water, this species will thrive in tapwater. A very shy species which will spend a lot of time hiding. It is best not to plant the tank too thickly or you will rarely see them. These very small fish are best fed on mosquito larvae, Cyclops and grindal worms. The male shows his finest coloration shortly before and during the spawning. Normally reddish brown, with light gray fins and a dark spot on the end of the dorsal. The edges of the dorsal and anal fins are light blue. This species is probably a cave breeder. Soft water is recommended for breeding, preferably filtered through peat. The breeding tank should have no substrate material. A small plant pot or similar will serve as a spawning area. The fry are reared in a manner similar to those of *P. deissneri* . Misc: Like *P. deissneri,* this is a rare fish, difficult to breed in the aquarium.

78

Genus *Malpulutta* Deraniyagala, 1937. *mal–* local word for flower; *pulutta–*local word for *Belontia signata).* Number of Species: 1. Size: About 70mm. Shape: Elongate. Fin Formation: Short ventrals (I/5), 8-10 hard and 4-6 soft dorsal rays, 13-17 hard and 7-11 soft anal rays. Dorsal and anal run to a point. The caudal runs to a thread-like point.

Malpulutta kretseri

Malpulutta kretseri Deraniyagala, 1937. Marbled Spike-tailed Gourami. *kretseri* - after the Sri Lankan, Juristen de Kretser, who discovered the fish before it

Malpulutta kretseri spawning under their nest.

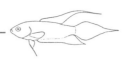

A brilliant male *Malpulutta kretseri* guarding his nest.

was described by Deraniyagala in 1937. First Description: Deraniyagala (1937): *Malpulutta kretseri* - a new species of fish from Ceylon. *Ceylon Journ. Sci.,* B. 20, pp.351-353. Natural Range: Sri Lanka - Kottowa Forest Reserve, 15 miles north-east of Galle. Ecology: Clear, running streams. Keeps mainly in vegetation near the banks. Capture area heavily vegetated; stream was approx. 1m wide and 25cm deep. As it was in the forest, sunlight barely reached the water surface. Water hardness 4 dH, pH 6.6. Water

temperature 27.5°C. Other fish in the stream included *Rasbora vaterifloris.* Total Length: about 70mm. Sex Determination: Sexes are easy to distinguish. Males are larger and more colorful. The fin pennants are much longer. Fin borders, especially those on the underside, show metallic blue. Females sombrely colored and barely 50mm in length. Gravid female darkens in color and develops

80

a narrow, light stripe from the mouth, over the back. Description: Fins: D VIII-X/4-6, A XIII-XVII/7-11, P 12, VI/5, C 13-15. Scales llr 29-30, dlr 9-10. Captive Care: This species likes to hide in dark spots so, if you want to see it now and again, you should not provide too many hiding places! A few rocks and cryptocorynes will be adequate. A mild flow in the water can be produced using an aerator and filter. Soft water is required for breeding; in hard water, the eggs will be killed by fungus. In breeding condition, the male builds a bubble nest under the leaf of an aquatic plant. The female darkens in color and swims around near to the nest. Then she holds her head downwards and swims, waggling, in the direction of the male. This is done only for a short time and she swims off again. This behavior may take place several times during a few days prior to spawning. Then, after a few trial pairings, the fish will suddenly begin to spawn, without any special preliminary displays. The initiative is always taken by the female, who swims to the male with open mouth, and prods him in the body. The male then bends his body somewhat and the fish swim

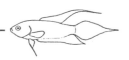

A pair of *Malpulutta kretseri* collected and photographed by Dr. Herbert R. Axelrod in Sri Lanka. Dr. Axelrod's photography in the jungle is the only record of the true colors of wild fish.

around each other in a circle. The female then swims into the curve of the male's body. This movement stimulates the male into taking her into a bodily embrace, holding her sideways; as spawning takes place, the fish sink slowly towards the substrate. The female lays her eggs on the anal fins of the male. The eggs are heavier than water but, due to the manner in which they are laid, most of them stay on the male's anal fin in a row. As the pair separates, the eggs will fall off and sink to the substrate. The female often removes eggs directly from the fins. After several pairings, the sunken eggs are collected by both sexes, the female usually starting first as she is first to recover from the pairing. About 4 eggs are produced per spawning act but it may be as many as 12. The female can bring the eggs to the bubble nest and is tolerated by the male for the whole time. Spawning may take up to two hours and further play may continue up to three hours more. When the male sees no more eggs he then drives the female away. The fry hatch in about 42 hours and are free swimming in 4 days. They can be reared on microscopic animals. Up to 150 juvenile fish can be produced from a brood.

Special Behaviour: This species, especially if shocked, can jump out of the water, so a good lid on the aquarium is essential. Displaying males show a strong color pattern and the fins become deep lilac.

Genus *Parosphromenus* Bleeker, 1879. *par* (Lat.) - similar *osphronemus,* from *Osphronemus goramy.* Number of Species: 2. Size: About 36mm. Shape: Elongate. Fin Formation: short ventrals (I/5), 8 hard and 7 soft dorsal rays; 8 hard and 8-9 soft anal rays.

Parosphromenus deissneri

Parosphromenus deissneri (Bleeker, 1859). Licorice Gourami. Other Names in the Literature: *Osphromenus deissneri* Bleeker, 1859; *Polyacanthus deissneri* Guenther, 1861; *Parosphromenus deissneri* Bleeker, 1879. First Description: Bleeker (1859): *Nat. Tijdschr. Ned. Ind.,* XVIII, p. 376, *Osphromenus deissneri.* Natural Range:

80km north-west of Singapore in a swampy forested area. After Bleeker: the island of Bangka off Sumatra; after Schmidt: Sumatra, near to Palembang. Ecology: In 3-4km long canals with dark brown water. The fish stay singly among reeds near the banks with their heads pointed diagonally towards the substrate. Total Length: About 36mm. Sex Determination: When displaying, the male is much more colorful than the female, with metallic, blue-green coloring to the lower fins. The female is yellowish-brown and altogether more

sombre. Description: Fins: D XIII/7, A XIII/8-9, P 2, V I/5, C 12. Scales: llr 30. Captive Care: This species may be kept in hard water. The aquarium should not be too thickly planted or you will not

Top: Male *Malpulutta kretseri.* Bottom, left: Male *Betta imbellis.* Bottom right: Female *Betta imbellis.*

see the fish very often. Breeding pairs should be placed in a tank of soft, mineral poor water, preferably without substrate material; just a cave for hiding. The fish may be fed with Cyclops, small mosquito larvae, grindals and nauplii. Males of the smaller labyrinth fishes are extremely attractively colored. It is best to put 8-10 specimens in a larger tank. In such a way the displaying fish can be observed and admired. Gravid females can be recognized by the swollen and lighter colored belly. These usually seek out a cave and stay there with their heads inclined towards the substrate. Usually a day later the male will join her and displays with spread fins and beautiful colors; he also holds his head downwards. Both sexes nibble at the ceiling of the cave as if cleaning it. During this behavior, the male bends his body and the female then swims into his bodily embrace. The female is not (or just a little) turned over. The first pairing is usually a trial and eggs are not laid until about an hour later. The first spawning often produces just one egg, laid on the male's anal fin. The male then releases his grip on the female and sinks a little. He then rises again in the same position. The female now takes the egg from the male's fin and attempts to stick it to the ceiling while the male watches carefully. If the egg falls off, both fish try to catch it and replace it. Up to 4 eggs per spawning act can be laid and about 50 eggs are finally produced. The male alone takes further care of the brood. The fry hatch approximately 45 hours after spawning and they are freely swimming in another five days. It is best to remove the fry to a separate rearing tank shortly before they begin free swimming. They should be fed on tiny aquatic life and may be slowly acclimatized to ordinary tap water. Although they grow quickly at first, at about 12mm their growth regularly seems to stagnate. In my experience the young fishes were sexually mature at seven months. Special Behavior: This species is very shy and in spite of careful observation, one rarely sees them obtaining air from the surface. Scientific examination of the labyrinth organ in this species is, to date, incomplete.

Spawning sequence of *Parosphromenus deissneri*. The male displays in front of the female in the photo above. The male in the photo, lower left is cleaning the spawning site. Lower right, the male prepares to wrap his body about the female.

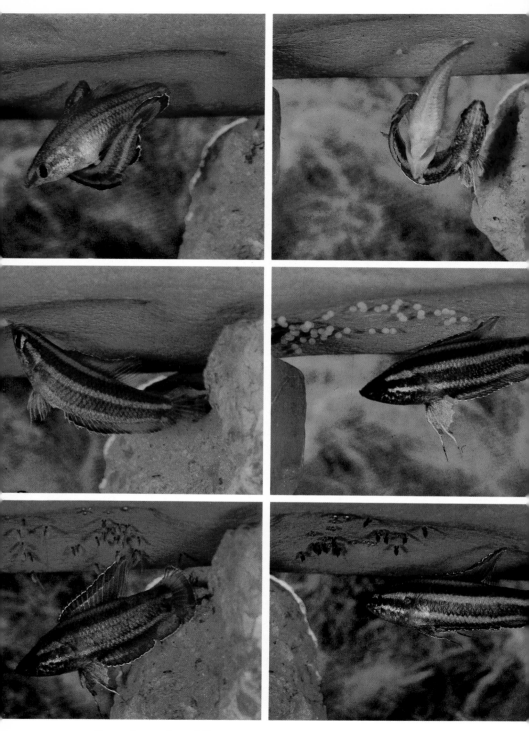

Spawning series of *Parosphromenus deissneri*. The pair embrace. The male remains stunned while the female picks the egg from his anal fin. The female places the egg on the top of the cave. The male alone guards the eggs and developing fry.

Parosphromenus paludicola

Parosphromenus paludicola Tweedie, 1952. First Description: Tweedie (1952): Notes on Malayan fresh-water fishes. *Bull. Raffles Mus.*, 24, pp. 63-95. Natural Range:

Marshy areas 3-400km north-west of Singapore. East coast of Malaya near to Trengganu.

Genus *Betta* Bleeker, 1850. *Betta* - taken from the Javanese name Wader bettah. Number of Species: Due to continuing current research, the exact number of species is not yet clear. Size: 50-120mm. Shape: Almost round in section; elongate. Fin Formation: Short ventrals (I/5), 1-2 hard and 6-10 soft dorsal rays; 1-5 hard and 18-30 soft anal rays. The anal is often very large in area.

The genus *Betta* has a basic division into bubble nest builders and mouthbrooders. A thorough conclusion as to whether these all belong in the same genus remains to be seen, especially as the mouthbrooding species have evolved a good deal further in their reproductive behavior.

Without question, the two groups are very similar in appearance and it can be surmised that they all arose from similar ancestors. Another problem is the large number of named *Betta* species to date. A shortage of living material has, to date, resolved few of these problems. In the following text, exact data can therefore

1	*B. anabatoides*	6	*B. picta*
2	*B. bellica*	7	*B. pugnax*
3	*B. brederi*	8	*B. splendens*
4	*B. fasciata*	9	*B. smaragdina*
5	*B. imbellis*	10	*B. taeniata*

only be given for those species in which the necessary information is available from aquarium sources. For completeness however, all known species are mentioned.

Betta akarensis

Betta akarensis Regan, 1909. First Description: Regan (1909): The Asiatic fishes of the family Anabantidae. *Proc. Zool Soc. London,* p. 779, fig. 77. Natural Range: Sarawak - Awak River. Total Length: about 52mm. Description: Fins: D 8, A l/27. Scales llr 31. Misc. Not normally imported for the aquarium trade.

Betta anabatoides

Betta anabatoides Bleeker, 1850. First Description: Bleeker (1850): Bijdrage tot de kennis der ichthyologische fauna van Midden en Oost Java. *Verh. Batav. Genootsch,* 23, p. 269. Natural Range: Singapore, Sumatra, Kalimantan (Borneo), Biliton. Ecology: According to Schmidt, near the banks of slow flowing waters. Total Length: to 120mm. Description: Fins: D l/7-9, All/25-30, P 13, V l/5. Scales

llr 31-34, dlr 10.5. Misc: A mouthbrooding species, seldom seen in the aquarium.

Betta balunga

Betta balunga Herre, 1940. First Description: Herre (1940): Notes on fishes in the Zoological Museum of Stanford University, VII. *Philippine Journ. Sc.,* vol. 72. Misc: Rarely seen in the aquarium.

Betta bellica

Betta bellica Sauvage, 1884. Slender Betta. *bellica* (Lat.) - pugnacious. First Description: Sauvage (1884): *Bull. Soc. Zool. France,* IX, p. 217, illustrated. Natural Range: Southern Malayan Peninsula (Perak); Thailand, 325km south of Bangkok. Ecology: According to Duncker, boggy areas of the Kinta River (tributary of the Perak River) and lakes with a muddy substrate that may be kilometers long in the rainy season, but dry up into 400m long lagoons in the dry

season. Mainly shallow and up to 2m deep. The water is very clear. Total Length: about 110mm. Sex Determination: Male more intensively colored. Description: Fins: D I/9-10, A II/27-30, V I/5, C 11. Scales: llr 35, dlr 9.5 Captive Care: This is a very delicate species. Further information on care is unfortunately not available. Misc: Rarely seen in the aquarium trade.

Betta bleekeri

Betta bleekeri Regan, 1909. Other Names in the Literature: *Betta picta* (not Valenciennes) Bleeker, 1879. First Description: Regan (1909): The Asiatic fishes of the family Anabantidae. *Proc. Zool. Soc. London,* p. 180. Description: Fins: D I/9, A II/27. Scales: llr 34. Misc: Rarely seen in the aquarium.

Top: Short finned *Betta anabatoides.* Center: A male *Betta taeniata.* Bottom: A male *Betta unimaculata.*

Betta brederi

Betta brederi Myers, 1935. Mouth-brooding Betta. First Description: Myers (1935): The mouth brooding fighting fish, *Betta brederi. The Aquarium,* vol. 3, no. 9, p. 210. Natural Range: Java and Sumatra. Total Length: after Roloff, 100mm, but may reach 120mm. Sex Determination: Sexes similar but male colored

slightly more intensively and with slightly longer finnage. Description: Fins: D II/8-9, A II/23-24, P 12, V I/5, C 9. Scales: IIr 29. Captive Care: Best kept in single pairs. The aquarium is best prepared as follows: substrate of fine

Top: Short-finned male *Betta splendens,* the type bred in Thailand for fighting purposes.
Center: Domesticated long-finned red Siamese Fighting Fish, *Betta splendens.*
Bottom: Rare chocolate *Betta.*
Photo by Dr. H. R. Axelrod.

Top: A male Mouthbrooding Fighting Fish, *Betta pugnax.* Bottom left:
The Javanese Mouthbrooding Fighting Fish, *Betta brederi.* Bottom right.
The Slender Fighting Fish, *Betta bellica.*

gravel, well planted in the background and with good hiding places (bogwood roots). Water temperature 24°C, no special requirements with regard to water quality. Feed with a variety of live food. Very fond of Enchytrae. Gravid females are recognizable by their swollen and lighter colored bellies. She will swim in the vicinity of the male and spread her fins, then swims backwards and forwards in front of the male. If the male is ready to spawn, he will follow the female to a chosen nest-site. The courtship procedure is then repeated time and again, often for several hours before the first embrace is made. The female pokes the male in the body with her mouth. The male then bends his body and lays on his side. Then the female swims into his bodily embrace from below. Trial pairings usually take place at first. Then the female releases one or two eggs, which usually lie on the male's anal fins. The female is released and she begins to collect the eggs together. After a few chewing motions, the female spits the eggs out in the direction of the male. At first the male takes no notice, so the collecting and spitting action is repeated. Eventually, the male snaps up the eggs and holds them in his mouth. Further spawnings take place over a

Betta brederi, the Mouthbrooding Betta. This male has a mouthful of eggs which he will retain throughout the brooding cycle. Photo by E. Roloff.

Betta bellica, the Slender Betta, which was collected and photographed by Dr. Herbert R. Axelrod in Thailand.

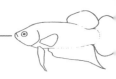

period of hours but eggs are not produced during every embrace. Egg numbers increase at each fruitful spawning but never more than 10 at a time. Altogether, up to 130 whitish eggs are produced. According to Roloff, the eggs turn oval shaped and become yellowish in color after a few days. After 11 days, the fry are developed, but they have a relatively large yolk sac. Roloff reports that the fry were free swimming in 12 days (artificial brooding in a glass container) and were fed with *Artemia* nauplii after the 13th day. Natural rearing has not yet been reported, the male usually eating the eggs by the third day. Special Behavior: *B. brederi* mainly stays near to the substrate. They seek out good hiding places so that one seldom sees them.

Betta coccina

Betta coccina Vierke, 1979. Dwarf Fighting Fish. *coccina* (Gr.) – red. First Description: Vierke (1979): *Betta coccina* nov. spec., ein neuer Kampffish von Sumatra. *Das Aquarium*, pp. 288-289. Natural Range: Jambi, central Sumatra. Ecology: Well

vegetated still and slow moving waters. Total Length: Male 45mm, female 39mm. Sex Determination: Male wine red in color. Darker head. Emerald green spot near upper middle of body. Dorsal with white border. Female uniform yellowish. Description: Fins: D II/7-10, A III/24-26, V I/5, C 11. Scales: llr 29-30 (2 on tail base). Captive Care: Minimum 50l capacity aquarium for this small fish. A 25cm water depth is adequate. The background can be planted with *Cryptocoryne* and a few larger stones can be laid over the substrate in the foreground. One or two pairs can be kept in such a set-up. Tapwater may be used for general care, but softer water is required for breeding. Water temperature about 25° C. Feed with small live-food. This species is a bubblenest builder (Schaller, 1979).

Betta foerschi

Betta foerschi Vierke, 1979. First Description: Vierke

(1979); *Betta anabantoides* and *Betta foerschi* spec. nov., zwei Kampffische aus Borneo. *Das Aquarium,* pp. 386-388. Natural Range: Mentyana river system, about 250km northwest of Banjarmasin, Kalimantan (south Borneo). Ecology: Marshy areas near to a fast running jungle stream. Very soft water with a pH of 4.8. Water temperature 24°C. Total Length: 65mm. Sex Determination: Male somewhat slimmer with larger fins. Gravid female has

swollen belly. Description: Fins: D I/8-9, A II/24, V I/5, C 11. Scales: IIr 31 (2-4 on the tail base). Captive Care: This is probably a bubble nest builder. It is best kept in single pairs in a minimum 50l capacity tank. Tapwater may be used but frequent water changing is recommended. Water temperature 24-28°C. Soft water is best used for breeding. This species is very shy and usually hides in dark corners.

Betta fasciata

Betta fasciata Regan, 1909. Striped Fighting Fish. *fasciata* (Lat.) - banded. First Description: Regan (1909): The Asiatic fishes of the family Anabantidae, *Proc. Zool. Soc. London,* p. 782. Natural Range: Sumatra. Ecology: In ponds and ditches, with murky, nearly coffee-colored waters. Total Length: After Arnold-Ahl, to 100mm. Sex Determination: According to Arnold-Ahl, spawning males

Above: A Striped Fighting Fish, *Betta fasciata* female. Below: A pair of Striped Fighting Fish, *Betta fasciata.* The male is the uppermost fish; the female is below him. Photos by Dave Roddy.

Above: *Betta coccina*, the Dwarf Fighting Fish, female. Below: *Betta coccina*, male. Photos by Horst Linke. Courtesy of Heiko Bleher.

The Boripat River in Thailand. This is the habitat of the *Betta pugnax*. The fast-moving river cuts the mud away from the bank. The plants growing into the edge of the water provide   an ideal refuge for the *Betta pugnax*. Photo by Dr. Rolf Geisler.

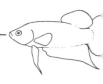

are indescribably beautiful, the females somber. Description: Fins: D I/9-10, A II/30. Scales IIr 34-36. Captive Care: A large, well planted tank is recommended. The fish should be kept in single pairs. The male builds a large bubble nest. The species has not been kept to the extent that concrete care and breeding information is available. Misc: Very similar to *B. bellica.*

Betta fusca

Betta fusca Regan, 1909. First Description: Regan (1909): The Asiatic fishes of the family Anabantidae, *Proc. Zool. Soc. London,* p. 780. Natural Range: Sumatra. Total Length: 82mm. Description: Fins: D 9, A II/21-24. Scales: IIr 31-32. Misc: Rarely imported.

Betta imbellis

Betta imbellis Ladiges, 1975, Peaceful Betta. imbellis (Lat.) - peaceful. First Description: Ladiges (1975) *DATZ,* XXVIII, p. 262. Natural Range: Malayan peninsula, north and south of Kuala Lumpur (Schaller), Ko Phuket and southern Thai islands at latitude 8°. Also Kuantan, Penang and Penang Island. Ecology: Swamp waters; according to Schaller, paddy fields, irrigation ditches and ponds. Water hardness 8-10 dH; pH 7, water temperature up to 34°C. The fish usually keep among water plants and vegetated marginal areas. Total Length: After Ladiges, 53mm. Sex Determination: Male, dark blue with long ventrals and large fins; red

Betta imbellis

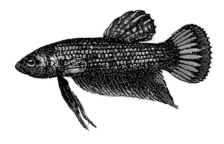

margin on caudal. Female, light brown and smaller. Description: Fins: D O-I/7-9, A III/22-25, C 11. Scales: IIr 27-30. Captive Care: Should preferably be kept in single pairs. A tank containing 20l plus is adequate. Temperature 25°C. A group can be kept in a large tank so that display behavior may be observed. This species is relatively peaceful, but territorial fighting will occur in the breeding season and fins may be damaged. *B. imbellis*

Two male Peaceful Bettas, *Betta imbellis,* displaying in front of a female. Photo by E. Rolfoff.

comes in a large number of color varieties. Breeding presents no particular problems. The species is very secretive and is not often seen in a well planted aquarium except during spawning when the male shows himself in his attractive courting colors. The bubble nest is built at the water surface. About 150 eggs are laid in each set of spawnings. Misc: This species may be crossed with *B. splendens.* The hybrids are beautifully colored and fertile.

Betta macrophthalma

Betta macrophthalma Regan, 1909. First Description: Regan (1909): The Asiatic fishes of the family Anabantidae, *Proc. Zool. Soc. London,* p.781. Natural Range: Singapore. Total Length: About 50mm. Description: Fins: D I/8, A I/23. Scales: llr 28. Misc: According to Smith, synonym of *B. taeniata.*

Betta macrostoma.

Betta macrostoma

Betta macrostoma Regan, 1909. First Description: Regan (1909): The Asiatic fishes of the family Anabantidae, *Proc. Zool. Soc. London,* p. 778.

Natural Range: Sarawak. Total Length: According to Regan, 80mm. Description: Fins: D 11, A 26. Scales: llr 32. Misc: To date, rarely imported.

The pugnaceous face of a male *Betta macrostoma.* Photo by Dr. Herbert R. Axelrod of a fish he collected in Brunei. No one has ever been able to keep this fish alive in captivity more than 90 days.

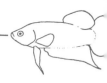

Left: A pair of Brunei Beauties, *Betta macrostoma*, collected and photographed by Dr. Herbert R. Axelrod. The fish shown spawning. Below: A young male *Betta macrostoma*. Each male of this species differs slightly from the next.

Betta picta

Betta picta (Cuvier and Valenciennes, 1846). Javan Mouth-brooding Fighter. Other Names in the Literature: *Panchax pictum* Cuvier and Valenciennes, 1846. First Description: Cuvier and Valenciennes (1846): *Histoire naturelle des poissons,* vol 18, p. 385 *(Panchax pictum).* Natural Range: Singapore, Sumatra, Java. Fins: D I/6-8, A II/18-22, P 12. Scales llr 28-30, dlr 9.5-10.5. Captive Care: May be kept in smaller aquaria. As their natural habitat is mountain streams, temperatures as low as 18°C are tolerated. Presumed to be a mouth-brooder.

A pair of *Betta picta,* the Javan Mouth-brooding Fighter, in spawning embrace.

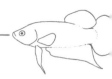

Betta pugnax

Betta pugnax (Cantor, 1849). Mouthbrooding Betta. *pugnax* (Lat.) - pugnaceous. Other Names in the Literature: *Macropodus pugnax* Cantor, 1849; *Betta pugnax* Guenther, 1861. First Description: Cantor (1849): *Journ. Roy. Asiatic Soc. Bengal,* XVIII, p. 1066 *(Macropodus pugnax).* Natural Range: Penang Island, Kuantan. According to Etzel, also in the area of Pajakumbuhl (West Sumatra).

Ecology: Shady and slow to faster moving waters under overhanging vegetation. Etzel reports it from a slow moving stream under a rocky escarpment. The stream was 20-30cm wide and 10-30cm

A pair of *Betta pugnax* preparing to spawn. Top, facing page: A male *Betta pugnax*. Photo by Dr. J. Vierke.

deep. Water temperature was 25°C. Total Length: According to Rachow, to 100mm. Sex Determination: The male's fins are all larger than those of the female and have longer pennants. The underside of the head is metallic green. The female is less colorful with smaller fins, the dorsal and tail fins are rounded and the ventrals short. Description: Fins: D I/7-9, A II/22-26, P 12, V I/5, C 11. Scales: llr 28-30. Captive Care: As described for *B. brederi* - also mouthbrooding. Misc: This beautiful Betta is, to date, rarely imported or bred. According to Ladiges (1972), this species should be called *B. picta* (Cuvier and Valenciennes, 1846). Further research is required before this can be substantiated.

Betta rubra

Betta rubra Perugia, 1893. First description: Perugia (1893): *Ann. Mus. Genova, (2) XIII, p. 242. Natural Range: Toba Lake, Sumatra. Description: Fins: D I/7, A III/21. Scales: llr 30. Misc: rarely imported.*

Betta splendens

Betta splendens Regan, 1909. Siamese Fighting Fish. *splendens* (Lat.) - splendid. Local Name: In Thailand, pla kat. Other Names in the Literature: *Macropodus pugnax* var. Cantor, 1850; *Betta pugnax* Bause, 1897; *B. pugnax* var. *trifasciata* Koehler, 1906; *B. pugnax* var. *rubra* Koehler, 1906; *B.*

trifasciata Mattha, 1909; *B. splendens* Regan, 1909; *B. rubra* Krueger, 1912. First Description: Regan (1909): The Asiatic fishes of the family Anabantidae, *Proc. Zool. Soc. London,* p. 782. Natural Range: Thailand. In view of the popularity of the Siamese Fighting Fish during the last 100 years, its exact original range is difficult to ascertain. Today, the fish may be found living wild in countries where they definitely never lived before. Ecology: In still and very slowly flowing waters, usually thickly vegetated. Total Length: To 60mm. Sex Determination: Male has large fins and intensive coloration. Female with smaller fins, sombre coloration and dark, longitudinal stripes outside the breeding season. Description: Fins: D I-II/8-10, A II-V/21-26, P 5, V I/5, C 11. scales: llr 27-31. Captive Care: The fighting properties of this fish are well known. They should be kept in single pairs in a relatively large, thickly planted aquarium (not under 20l capacity). More than one pair can be kept in a very large tank, but there is always the danger that the males will severely damage

A male *Betta splendens* spawning with a *Macropodus*.

A Rainbow Marble *Betta splendens* with an unusual combination of colors. Photo by Al Liebtrau.

each other's fins during territorial fighting. No special requirements regarding water quality. Temperature around 25°C. Feed with a variety of live and dry foods. The male builds a bubble nest on the water surface, usually under floating leaves of aquatic plants. At this time, he is particularly aggressive and will even drive the female away.

The mating of a very beautiful color variety of *Betta splendens*. This peach color has been fixed but the strain has never become popular.

Above: A red "Butterfly" or variegated type male Siamese Fighting Fish. The true "Butterfly" has color on the outside edges of the fins with clear where this fish shows red in its fins. Photo by Gene Lucas. The same is true of the "Butterfly" *Betta* shown below. Photo by Jim Sonnier.

The gravid female is easily recognized by the swollen, light-colored belly. In addition, the genital opening is swollen and light colored. If both sexes are ready, a few trial pairings will first take place. After each trial pairing the male is again aggressive and drives his partner off. As soon as eggs appear, he changes his attitude. He guides her towards the nest, where she will prod him in the side with her snout. The female waggles her body in front of the male; the male curves his body and takes the female in a bodily embrace. He turns the female so that her underside is facing upwards. As the female spawns, her body is S shaped. As the eggs appear, the male begins to loosen his grip. Some of the eggs will start to sink towards the substrate. These eggs are collected by the male and taken to the nest. It is worth comment that sometimes eggs will stay on the female's anal fins and the male will not collect these until they fall off. The female also begins to help collecting the fallen eggs, turning stones and searching every inch of the substrate. The eggs are brought by both partners to the nest, but the male always has priority of entry. Each pairing produces about 40

eggs - making a total of about 200. The male looks after the brood aggressively. The fry hatch in about 24 hours They have a large, whitish yolk sac and they begin to sink; the male continually collects them and returns them to the nest. In another 2 days, the fry are free swimming. Vierke reported that, if the male was removed, the female would continue to carefully look after the brood. Special Behavior: Kuehme (1961) reported an unusual aspect of brooding behavior. As fry became free swimming, the male would stay directly under the water surface and vibrate his pectoral fins. The result was that all fry swam to him, even from as far as 40cm away, and stayed in the area of his mouth. While continuing to vibrate his fins, the fry were gathered in his mouth and spat into the nest or into a shady spot. Misc: According to Smith, the veil-finned fighting fish varieties were known in Thailand in 1900. It is interesting to note that in Thailand, these are known as pla kat khmer - Fighting Fish from the Land of Khmer (Kampuchea). How these varieties arose however, is unknown. They could have arisen through mutations or through selective breeding.

110

The true "Tutweiler" Butterfly Betta. It has disappeared as a strain. Photo by Dr. Axelrod.

A magnificent male Siamese Fighting Fish, *Betta splendens*. The black edging on its anal and caudal fins makes this an outstanding example.

Today, these fighting fish are available in a great variety of colors and are one of the most popular of all aquarium fish species. In order to preserve the male's fine finnage, as soon as the juveniles are recognizable as males they should be reared separately. In Thailand, whisky bottles are used for this; in Europe, jam-jars. However, this is not recommended and each fish should be kept in a small, plastic or glass tank with a minimum capacity of 11l. More room will allow for a better fin development. In Thailand, the fish are used for competitive fighting. Bets are placed on the competing fish. Fish may be freshly captured from the wild, or aquarium bred specimens may be used. The competing fish are proudly exhibited to the audience before they fight; bets are taken, then the fish are introduced to each other. Happily, this sport is no longer as popular as it once was.

Betta smaragdina

Betta smaragdina Ladiges, 1972. Emerald Betta. *smaragdina* - emerald. First Description: Ladiges (1972): *DATZ*, XXV, p. 190. Natural

Range: Thailand east of Korat, near to the Laotian border. Ecology: The fish were found in 30cm deep footprints of water buffalos, in an almost dried out paddy field. It is probable that the fish originated from the water used to irrigate the paddy. Total Length: about 70mm. Sex Determination: The males have larger fins. The ventrals are long and red, with white tips. The female is brownish in color with dark diagonal stripes; the fins are smaller and shorter. Description: Fins: D I-II/7-9, A IV-V/22-26. Scales: llr 31-35 Captive Care: *B. smaragdina* is a relatively peaceful Betta and several specimens may be kept together in an aquarium of suitable size. They are also well suited for a community tank. Care is as described for *B. splendens*. It also builds a bubble nest for spawning and the male can become very aggressive in the breeding season. It is therefore recommended, that if

Betta smaragdina.

breeding is contemplated in a community tank, adequate space is provided so that the male(s) have suitably sized territories. Roloff bred this species with a water hardness of 8 dH and pH 7. The water temperature was 26°C. The fish were especially ready to spawn after a water change. The fry hatched in 24 hours. Misc: This species was found by Schaller and has not been found anywhere else. It must now be regarded as disappeared. Crossings with other bubble-nest builders in the *Betta splendens* complex have produced fry which soon died. Chromosome examinations have proven that this is a species in its own right and not a race of *B. splendens*

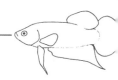

A male *Betta smaragdina* catching an egg as the female still remains stunned from the spawning embrace.

Betta taeniata Regan 1909. *taeniata* (Gr.) - banded. Local Name: In Thailand; pla krim hua mong. Other Names in the Literature: *Betta trifasciata* Karoli, 1882.*Betta macrophthalma* Fowler, 1934. First Description: Regan (l909): The Asiatic fishes of the family Anabantidae, *Proc. Zool. Soc. London,* p. 781. Natural Range: Senah River, Sarawak. According to Smith, also Sumatra. Those described by Smith however are supposed to have originated in

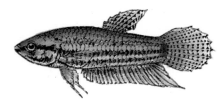

Nakhornratchsima in Thailand and also from Chanthaburi, southeast of Bangkok. Roloff found it on the island of Ko Samui in 1956, in the hills between Trang and Phatalung. Linke also reports it from Kota Tinggi, about 80 km north of Singapore. Ecology: Smith reported it in Klong Nakon Noi, a clear, vegetated stream which runs through Nakhornratchsima. The species was found living together with *Trichopsis,* *Trichogaster, Nandus, Rasbora* and *Aplocheilus* species. A specimen was found in a mountain stream near Ban Ang on the Kao Sabap in south-east Thailand, together with *Trichopsis* species. Roloff caught the specimens in relatively fast moving waters near to the banks among rushes. Total Length: about 80mm. Sex Determination: Barely discernible. Only the gravid female shows a swollen abdomen. Description: Fins: D l/7-9, A ll/20-25, P 12-14, C 11, V l/5. Scales: llr 28-30, dlr 9.5-10.5. General Care: The care of this large, colorful fighting fish is problem free. The aquarium substrate should consist of fine grade shingle and be well planted. The fish are relatively shy and usually hide among the plants and roots at the bottom. One can keep several specimens in a large tank. The males do not show the continual aggressiveness as seen in *B. splendens.* Only when breeding will both sexes defend the nesting area. According to Kuenzer breeding poses no special problems. One of his females spawned regularly with one or another of two males every 4-5 days. Before pairing, both sexes circle each other with spread fins. They defend their territory by threatening any encroacher with the body held in a diagonal position. If this does not work the fish will then ram the offender with its snout and drive it off. When ready to pair, the female prods the male in the side with her snout. The male then bends his body and sinks below her. The female then swims into his bodily embrace. The eggs are laid on the anal fins of the male where they stay until the embrace is loosened. Each spawning produces about 20 eggs which are whitish in color and heavier than water. When the female is released from the male's embrace she takes up the eggs from his anal fin and holds them in her mouth. A little while later she will attempt to give them over to the male after he has got

Betta edithae, named to honor the late Edith Korthaus. This species was previously known as *Betta taeniata*.

himself into a normal posture. She will spit the eggs out in front of the male's mouth. He reacts relatively slowly and she may have to retrieve the eggs and repeat the process several times before he accepts them all. Then the next pairing takes place and so on. The whole breeding process takes several hours. Then the sexes separate and the male goes into hiding with the brood in his mouth. The fry are released in 8-9 days and are immediately independent. There is no further parental care and indeed, the parents may then eat them if they are not separated. Misc: This species is, to date, rarely kept in the aquarium.

Betta trifasciata

Betta trifasciata Bleeker, 1850. First Description: *Verh. Bat. Gen.,* 23 (8) p. 12; Java. According to Smith, a synonym of *B. taeniata.* Natural Range: Kalimantan (Borneo); in the Bongon, Howong and Kajan Rivers. Total Length: about 82mm. Description (after Goldstein): Fins: D 0/7-9, A 0/27-30. Scales: llr 32-33. Misc: Rarely seen in the aquarium.

Betta unimaculata

Betta unimaculata, the One-spot Betta, was originally described by Popta in 1905 (*Notes Leyden Museum, XXV, page 184*) as *Paraophicephalus unimaculatus.* Its range is reported as Kalimantan (Borneo) from small streams and tributaries of the Bongon, Howong and Kajan Rivers. Horst Linke first collected the fish near Tawau in Sabah, Borneo. The first spawning report of the fish is to be found in *Tropical Fish Hobbyist Magazine,* November, 1981 beginning on page 18. This is a large *Betta* growing to about 4½ inches. Popta reported it only grows to about 3¼ inches. The males carry the eggs and their enlarged gular (lower throat) area enlarges when filled with eggs. The male hides during the egg incubation period.

In the literature, the following *Betta* species are also mentioned but are, at present, not proven species: *B. macrodon* Regan; *B. ocellata* Beaufort, 1933; *B. patoti* Weber and Beaufort.

One-spot Betta *Betta unimaculata,* during their spawning embrace.

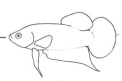

The male One-spot Betta, *Betta unimaculata,* with the distended throat pouch filled with eggs. Even with his pouch so distended, the male continued to spawn.

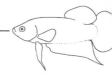

Above: As you can see from the
clump of eggs laying on the bottom,
the eggs are not round.

Facing page: The male *Betta
unimaculata* quickly snatches the
eggs to incubate them orally.

Genus *Trichopsis* -
Canestrini, 1860. *Trichopsis* -
Trichopus-like (*Trichopus*,
synonym of *Trichogaster*).
Number of Species: 3. Size:
50-80mm. Shape: elongate.
Fin Formation: long, thread-
like ventrals (I/5), 2-4 hard and
6-8 soft dorsal rays; 5-9 hard
and 19-28 soft anal rays. The
anal is large in area.

spec. Arnold, 1914; *Ctenops
pumilus* Arnold, 1936;
Trichopsis pumilus Stoye,
1948. First Description: Arnold
(1936), Wochenschriften Aqu.
Terrkd., vol. 33, 11. (1937):
Zool. Anz., vol. 117 5/6, pp.
116-117. Natural Range:
Thailand, Kampuchea.
Ecology: Found in slow
moving waters with thick
vegetation. Very soft and
mineral-poor water with a pH
around 6.5. Total Length:
about 70mm. Sex
Determination: Males have
larger dorsal and anal fins
than the females. In gravid
females, the rear part of the
ovaries are easily seen with a
good back light. It may be
seen directly under the swim
bladder as a light, elongate
shape. Gravid females are
also much plumper than the
males. Description: Fins: D
III/7-8, A V/20-25, P 10-11, V
I/5, C 13-14. Scales: llr 27-28,
dlr 9. Captive Care: This little
labyrinth is not suitable for the
community tank, but possible
if the other fish are of similar
size. However, it is best to
keep this species in single

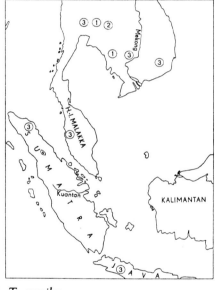

1. *T. pumilus*
2. *T. schalleri*
3. *T. vittatus*

Trichopsis pumilus

Trichopsis pumilus (Arnold,
1936). Pygmy Gourami
pumilus-dwarf. Other Names
in the Literature: *Ctenops*

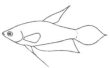

Trichopsis pumilus, the Pygmy Gourami (not to be confused with the Dwarf Gourami). The male wraps his body about the female immediately under the leaf in which the bubblenest has been built.

pairs or in small numbers up to say, 8. They do not require a large tank. A 10l tank with a water temperature of 25°C is adequate for breeding purposes. A large-leafed aquatic plant (*Cryptocoryne* or *Anubias* for example), or a cave should be provided. This species prefers to spawn at middle depth or near to the substrate. The male very rarely builds a bubble nest at the water surface. The nest is built very quickly before the pairing. The male swims backwards and forwards to the female while nest building and displays with spread fins. At this time, one can hear croaks or growls emitted by the fish. The gravid female eventually swims with the male, or sometimes on her own, to the nest. Then the pair swim around each other with bodies bent, until the male takes the female into his embrace. At first, only trial pairings take place. With a real spawning, one can see the male making shivering

Top, left: A young male Pygmy Gourami, *Trichopsis pumilus*. Bottom, left: *Trichopsis vittatus.*

motions with his body as he gives up his sperm. At the same time, the female gives out her eggs in the form of egg-packets containing two or three eggs. These egg-packets are fertilized in the cloud of milt, then almost immediately snapped up by the male who carries them straight into the nest. Each group of eggs is covered with a further layer of bubbles. While the male busies himself with the nest, the female comes to start the spawning act. Spawning takes place at decreasing intervals over a period of about two hours and a good female can produce up to 400 eggs. Very occasionally, it can happen that the egg-packet falls apart and the eggs fall singly to the substrate. These eggs are collected up by the female but she is not allowed near the nest so she has to spit the eggs towards the male from a short distance. He will then take these eggs to the nest. After spawning, only the male is concerned with the brood.

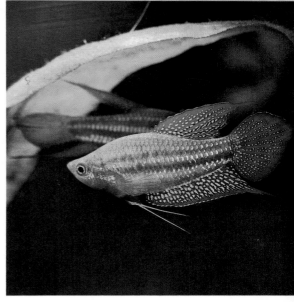

Top, right: *Trichopsis schalleri* male tending his bubblenest. Bottom right: A hybrid crossed from *T. schalleri* and *T. pumilus*.

125

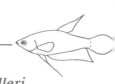

The fry hatch in about 24 hours. They possess a large, whitish yolk sac and hang in the nest, tail downwards. After three days, the fry are free swimming and must be fed with microscopic water life. Special Behavior: Displaying (especially rival) males, growl quite intensively. Spawning may occur some distance from the nest. Sometimes the pair choose a spot near to the nest, where they meet for each spawning.

Trichopsis schalleri

Trichopsis schalleri Ladiges, 1962. Three-striped Croaking Gourami *schalleri* - after the discoverer of the species, Schaller, Freiburg. First Description: Ladiges (1962): *DATZ*, XV, p. 102. Natural Range: According to Schaller, in the area of Nam-Mun, Korat, Thailand (about 220km north-east of Bangkok). Ecology: All kinds of thickly vegetated waters. Total

A beautiful *Trichopsis schalleri* male.

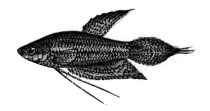

Length: about 60mm. Sex Determination: As described for *T. pumilus* . Description: Fins: D III/6-7, A VIII-IX/19-22, V I/5. Captive Care: As described for *T. pumilus,* but better suited to the community tank as they are larger. Special Behavior: Also croaks when excited. Crosses with *T. pumilus* (Richter) and *T. vittatus* (Vierke).

Trichopsis vittatus

Trichopsis vittatus (Cuvier and Valenciennes, 1831). Croaking Gourami *vittatus* (Lat.) - banded. Local Name: Generally pla Krim; in the Chantabun region, pla kat pa. Other Names in the Literature: *Osphromenus vittatus* Cuvier and Valenciennes, 1831; *Trichopus striatus* Bleeker, 1859; *Trichopsis striatos* Canestrini, 1860; *Osphromenus striatus*

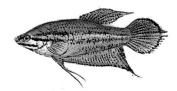

Guenther, 1861; *Ctenops striatus* Bleeker, 1878; *C. nobilis* (not McClelland, 1844) Vaillant, 1893; *Trichopsis harrisi* Fowler, 1934; *T. vittatus* Fowler, 1934. First Description: Cuvier and Valenciennes (1831): *Histoire naturelle des poissons,* 7, p. 387 *(Osphromenus vittatus).* Natural Range: Vietnam, Kampuchea, Thailand, Malaya and the Greater Sunda Islands. Ecology: Densely vegetated waters of many kinds. Total Length: about 80mm Sex Determination: Males have larger fins. Female has plumper, lighter colored belly. Description: Fins: D II-IV/6-8, A VI-VIII/24-28, P 11, V I/5. Scales: llr 28-29. Captive Care: May be kept in a community tank. No special requirements regarding water hardness. In smaller tanks, only a single male of this species should be kept, otherwise serious territorial fighting will develop. The breeding of this species is problem-free. Unlike the previously described species, *T. vittatus* often builds his bubble nest directly at the water surface, usually under or next to a floating leaf. The ripe female shows a strongly swollen abdomen. This species also produces egg-packets, but consisting of 4-6

127

Ctenops nobilis collected by Heiko Bleher in India in 1987. Photo by Horst Linke.

Facing page: A spawning series of *Trichopsis vittatus.* The pair embrace in typical anabantoid fashion. As the eggs are released, the male snaps them up immediately.

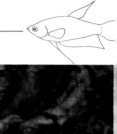

A male *Trichopsis vittatus* displays before a female.

eggs. Single spawning acts only take a couple of seconds and the egg packet literally shoots out of the female's genital opening. The male turns quick as lightning and snaps up the egg-packet in his mouth, sometimes still hanging onto the female with his tail-fin. The male's body is bent into an S shape. If the egg-packets fall apart, the female will help collect the eggs and is even allowed to spit them into the nest. Up to 600 eggs may be expected from larger specimens.

Special Behavior: The croaking noise made by excited fish is so loud that one can hardly miss it. The noise is mainly made by males displaying to each other in threat behavior. Misc: Individuals from different areas show a variety of patterns. The shoulder spot is not seen on all examples, but mainly those from Thailand and southern Vietnam. The number of lateral stripes varies between 3 and 4.

Genus *Ctenops* McClelland, 1844. Ctenops. ktenos, kteis (Gr.) - comb; ops (Gr.) eye. The name is used to indicate the comb-like edging to the pre-orbital scales. Number of Species: 1. Size: 75-100mm. Shape: Elongate. Fin Formation: Short ventrals (I/5), 5-7 hard and 7-8 soft dorsal rays, 9-10 hard and 24-28 soft anal rays.

Ctenops nobilis

Ctenops nobilis McClelland, 1844. *nobilis* (Lat.) - recognizable. Other Names in the Literature: *Osphromenus nobilis* Day, 1878. First Description: McClelland (1844): *Journ. Nat. Hist. Calcutta*, V, p. 281 pl. XXI, Fig

1. Natural Range: According to Ladiges, Assam Raimona, Goalpara District, Janali River. Total Length 75mm (Regan), 100mm (Rachow). Description: Fins: D V-VII/7-8, A IV-V/23-28. Scales: llr 29-33. Regan described the fish as brownish with dark lateral stripes and scattered flecks; an eye-spot

on the upper part of the tail-base. Captive Care: Due to its rarity in captivity, no data are available. Misc: This species seems to be scarce, even in its natural habitat. A good illustration of this species may be found in *Fish Ind.*, p. 372, pl. LXXVIII, fig 5 (Day 1878 under *Osphromenus nobilis*).

Subfamily Trichogasterinae
Genus *Trichogaster* Bloch, 1801. Trichogaster. *trichos,* (Gr.) - hair; *gaster* (Gr.) - belly. Named after the extended ventrals. Number of Species: 4. Size: 120-200mm. Shape: Laterally flattened, elongate. Fin Formation: long, thread-like ventrals (I/2-4), 3-9 hard and 7-11 soft dorsal rays, 9-14 hard and 25-40 soft anal rays. The caudal is slightly forked.

Trichogaster leeri

Trichogaster leeri (Bleeker, 1852). Pearl Gourami. *leeri* - after van Leer, a Dutch doctor (colleague of Bleeker). Other Names in the Literature: *Trichopodus trichopterus* Cantor, 1850; *Trichopus leerii* Bleeker, 1852; *Osphromenus trichopterus* var. *leerii* Guenther, 1861; *Trichopodus leeri* Regan, 1909. First

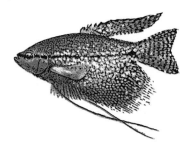

Description: Bleeker (1852): *Naturk. Tijdschr. Nederl. Ind.,* III, p. 577. Natural Range: Malayan Peninsula, Sumatra and Borneo. Ecology: Shallow, thickly vegetated ponds and lakes. Ladiges reported that they were seldom found in free water. He found them in stagnant waters with substrate consisting of meters thick decaying vegetation, and only shallow free water at the surface. Total Length: about 120mm. Sex Determination: Males generally more slender with flowing pennants to the dorsal and anal fins. In breeding dress, with blood red throat and breast. Female somewhat smaller and more sombrely colored. Plumper in the belly. Description: Fins: D V-VII/8-10, A XII-XIV/25-30, P 9, V I/3-4. Scales llr: 44-50. Captive Care: In view of its size, this species should be kept in well planted, larger aquaria. Initially shy fish will soon begin to show themselves in such a set-up. There are no special requirements regarding water quality. Feed with a variety of live and dry foods. The male builds a relatively large bubble nest, mostly without the use of plant material. The eggs in the nest are covered with fine bubbles (opercular aeration).

2,000 eggs per spawning is not unusual. Special Behavior: Males of *T. leeri* often build a bubble nest without spawning. They spit grains of sand in the nest and, over a period of time these can develop into quite a large sand hill under the nest. Like many cichlid species, the males also participate in mouth combat. They face each other and touch each other with their feeler-like ventrals. Then they swim slowly towards each other and bite into each other's mouth . They then release each other and start the process again from the beginning. Misc: This labyrinth is one of the most beautiful of all fishes and is nearly always available from suppliers. In spite of its size, it is relatively peaceful - even during the spawning season.

Facing page, top: Preserved specimens of the rare *Ctenops nobilis* which was first brought back alive by Heiko Bleher. Below: A male Pearl Gourami, *Trichogaster leeri*.

A spawning sequence of the Pearl Gourami, *Trichogaster leeri*. The male builds a bubble nest, entices the female to spawn, wraps his body around her under the nest and the huge spawn (averages 2,000 eggs) floats up into the nest. These are very peaceful fish.

Trichogaster microlepis

Trichogaster microlepis (Guenther, 1861). Moonlight Gourami. *microlepis* - with small scales. Local Name: In Thailand: pla gadi nang. Other Names in the Literature: *Ospromenus microlepis* Guenther, 1861; *Trichopus microlepis* Sauvage, 1881; *T. parvipinnis* Sauvage, 1883; *Deschauenseeia chryseus* Fowler, 1934. First Description: Guenther (1861): *Catalogue Fish. Brit. Mus.* III, p. 385. Natural Range: Kampuchea, Thailand. Ecology: According to

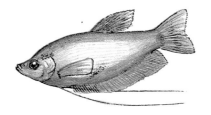

Meinken: in standing and slow flowing waters. Total Length: about 180mm. Sex Determination: Only positively possible with adult specimens. Male slimmer than female and with longer dorsal fins. The male's ventrals are orange to red; those of the female usually yellowish. The female has a relatively plumper belly. When spawning, the male shows dark lateral stripes from the gills to the tail base.

Description: Fins: D III-IV/7-10, A X-XI/34-40. Scales: llr 58-65. Captive Care: The Moonlight Gourami is often referred to as a silver fish without a pattern. Large examples, especially males show a bluish shimmer and are particularly beautiful. Due to their large size, a spacious aquarium is required. A well planted tank, of not less than 100l capacity is recommended. The male builds a nest on the water surface, consisting mainly of pieces of vegetation. Whole water plants may be ripped out and used. Bubbles are used among the vegetation to hold it together. The finished nest can be 25 cm in diameter and up to 15cm thick! A concentrated bubble nest is usually made somewhere near the center of this mass. Spawning behavior is similar to that of *T. leeri* . The fish stay under the nest so that the floating eggs end up in the right place; however many of the eggs are collected by the male and spat into the nest. The eggs are covered with more tiny bubbles (pressed through the gills). This species produces as many as 5,000 eggs in a group of spawnings. The fish should be fed with a variety of live and dry foods. Misc: The Moonlight Gourami

is called pla kadi nang in Thailand. Nang means wife or woman. This name resulted in the fact that the silvery fish was thought to be the female of *T. trichopteris*. Other *Trichogaster* species are known simply as pla kadi.

The Moonlight Gourami, *Trichogaster microlepis*, collected and photographed by Dr. Herbert R. Axelrod. Below: A typical nest built by *Trichogaster microlepis*.

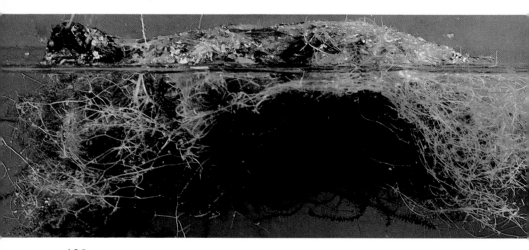

Top, left: *Trichogaster pectoralis.* Top, right: A school of *Trichogaster pectoralis* youngsters. Bottom, left: A Moonlight Gourami, *Trichogaster microlepis.* Bottom, right: A great many Moonlight Gouramis develop with deformities probably because they have all been inbred from the single pair Dr. Axelrod brought in many years ago.

Trichogaster pectoralis

Trichogaster pectoralis
(Regan, 1909). Snakeskin
Gourami. *pectoralis* -
appertaining to the large
pectoral fins. Local Name: In
Thailand: pla salid and pla bai
mai. Other Names in the
Literature: *Trichopodus
pectoralis* Regan, 1909;
Trichogaster pectoralis Smith,
1933. First Description: Regan
(1909): The Asiatic Fishes of
the Family Anabantidae, *Proc.
Zool. Soc. London,* p. 784
(Trichopodus pectoralis).

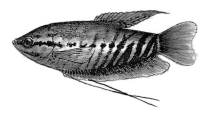

Natural Range: Thailand and
Malayan Peninsula. Ecology:
According to Meinken: in slow
flowing and standing waters.
Total Length: to 200mm. Sex
Determination: Male slimmer
than female and with longer
flowing fin pennants. Female
dorsal fins rounded and
shorter. Female with plumper
belly. Description: D VII/10-11,
A IX-XI/36-38, P 11, V I/2.
Scales: llr 55-63. Captive Care:
In view of its large size, this
species cannot be regarded
as an ideal fish for the home

aquarium. It is therefore not
seen a great deal in the trade.
A well planted tank of not less
than 100l is recommended.
The fish are very shy and
require good hiding places. It
is best to keep just a single
pair in a tank; they are more
likely to breed if not disturbed
by other fish. They will feed on
a variety of live and dry foods.
When displaying, they often
show a kind of mouth combat,
though not like that of cichlids,
more like that of the Kissing
Gourami. The fish face each
other and swim slowly
together. The lips are then
pressed into contact and
quickly released. The male
builds a relatively small bubble
nest under plants or pieces of
vegetation. It is usually 6-8cm
in diameter and about 0.5-1cm
thick. After a few trial pairings,
the fish spawn directly under
the nest and regular clouds of
tiny, amber-colored eggs are
produced; these nearly all end
up in the nest. Any eggs that
do not make it into the nest
are not collected. After
spawning, the fish are no
longer concerned with the
brood (after some of my own
observations in an 80l tank).
The fry hatch in about 36
hours and are ignored by the
parents. After a further three
days the fry are free swimming
and must be fed. As many as

Trichogaster pectoralis, the Snakeskin Gourami.

5,000 fry are produced from a spawning process. With good feeding and frequent water changes, the fry can reach 5cm in 8 weeks. Special Behavior: Mueller (1972) reports that this species spits above the water surface during nest building. Misc: According to Hugh Smith, there is a particularly large sized local race of this species in the Supanburi district of Central Thailand (Klong Kok Kamyan). It was reported that these fish are as thick as a man's hand. They are regarded by the locals as good to eat. Juvenile specimens have a zig-zag line from the eye to the tail base. At the end of this line, there is a 6mm wide black spot. The line may still be seen in more mature specimens, but it will completely disappear during spawning behavior.

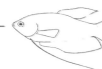

Trichogaster trichopterus

Trichogaster trichopterus (Pallas, 1770). The two following subspecies are known:

Trichogaster trichopterus trichopterus (Pallas, 1770). Three-spot Gourami. *trichopterus* (Gr.) - hair-like fin

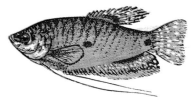

(ventrals). Local Name: In Thailand: pla kadi or pla kadi mor; in north Thailand: pla salark or pla salaring. Other Names in the Literature: *Labrus trichopterus* Pallas, 1770; *Trichogaster trichopterus* Bloch and Schneider, 1801; *Trichopodus trichopterus* Lacepede, 1801; *Trichopus trichopterus* Cuvier and Valenciennes, 1831; *T. sepat* Bleeker, 1845, *Osphromenus siamensis* Guenther, 1861; *O. trichopterus* Bleeker, 1865; *O. trichopterus* var. *Koelreuteri* Guenther, *O. trichopterus* var. *cantoris* Guenther; *Trichopus siamensis* Sauvage, 1881; *T. cantoris* Sauvage, 1884; *Trichopodus maculatus* Vipulya, 1923; *Osphromenus*

140

saigonensis Borodin, 1930. First Description: Pallas (1770): *Spicilegia zoologica,* pt. 8, p. 45. Natural Range: Southern Vietnam, Kampuchea, Thailand, Malayan Peninsula, Sunda Islands. Ecology: Rivers, canals. ditches, lakes, ponds and swamps. They stay mainly in thickly vegetatated parts where they are safer from predatory fish and birds. Total Length: about 120mm Sex Determination: Male slimmer and with larger, flowing dorsal fin than female. Female with rounded dorsal and plumper belly. Description: Fins: D VII-IX/8-10, A X-XII/33-38, P 9-10, V I/3-4. Scales: llr 40-52. Captive Care: As described for *T. leeri* . About 4,000 eggs per spawning. Special Behavior: This species has been observed to spit water after spawning (Richter) and to catch prey by spitting (Vierke). Strong color change can occur, depending on the mood. When pairing, the male swims up and down, thereby stroking his partner's belly, just before he takes her into his bodily embrace. Miller (1964) describes this as rubbing. This brown subspecies is often described as the wild form but this is not proven. Like the following

Trichogaster trichopterus, the Three-spot Gourami. This is a wild-caught fish from Indodnesia photographed and collected by Dr. Herbert R. Axelrod.

forms, this species will greedily eat Hydra when hungry. They have a reputation as hydra destroyers.

Trichogaster trichopterus sumatranus Ladiges, 1933. Blue Gourami *sumatranus* - from Sumatra. This blue form was brought in large numbers to Hamburg by a sailor in 1933. It is therefore most probably a wild form.

Trichogaster trichopterus sumatranus form Cosby. Cosby Gourami. Cosby - after the American breeder. This is a mutation of *T. t. sumatranus,* produced in the tanks of American breeder Cosby.

Trichogaster trichopterus sumatranus form Gold Gourami. Another mutation of *T. t. sumatranus* which appeared in 1970. Exact origin of the form is unknown.

141

Trichogaster trichopterus sumatranus form Silver Gourami. A further mutation of *T. t. sumatranus* which appeared in 1970. Further details on the origin are not available. This is less attractive than the preceding forms and is not seen so often in the trade. Due to the number of forms already available, it is not unlikely that new forms will appear.

Above: A color variety of *Trichogaster trichopterus*. This strain is available only in Brazil. Facing page: A golden variety of *Trichogaster trichopterus*. Photo above by Harald Schultz.

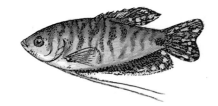

Above: Threespot Blue Gourami, *Trichogaster t. trichopterus.* Below: The Blue Gourami, *Trichogaster t. sumatranus.*

Above: The Marbled Blue Gourami also known as the Cosby Gourami. It is a *Trichogaster t. sumatranus* variety. Below, left: Golden *T.t. sumatranus*. Bottom, right: *T.t. sumatranus,* silver variety. 145

These young Cosby Gouramis are also known as Opaline Gouramis. They are members of the *Trichogaster trichopterus* group. The fish shown below have been sold as "Heavenly Blue" Gouramis, but they are nothing more than *Trichogaster trichopterus* in a new color form domestically produced. Upper photo by Arend van den Nieuwenhuizen.

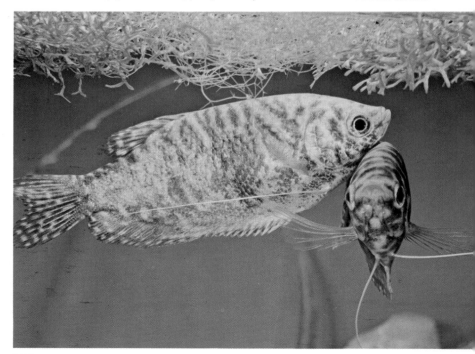

Genus *Colisa* Cuvier and Valenciennes, 1831. *Colisa* – taken from the local name, kholisha. Number of Species: 5. Size: 42–100mm. Shape: Laterally flattened, lightly elongate to elongate. Fin Formation: Long, thread-like ventrals (1), 12-19 hard and 7-14 soft dorsal rays, 15-20 hard and 11-20 soft anal rays.

Colisa chuna

Colisa chuna (Hamilton-Buchanan, 1822). Honey Dwarf Gourami. Local Name: In India: chuna. Other Names in the Literature: *Trichopodus chuna* Hamilton-Buchanan, 1822; *Colisa chuna* Cuvier and Valenciennes, 1831; *Trichogaster chuna* Day, 1878; *Colisa chuna* Myers, 1923. First Description: Hamilton-Buchanan (1822): *Fish. Ganges,* pp. 120-372 *(Trichopodus chuna).* Natural Range: The Brahmaputra basin, India-Assam (Dibrugarh to Hugli near Calcutta), Bangladesh, around Dacca. Ecology: Soft, mineral-poor, thickly vegetated waters. Total Length: about 42cm. Sex Determination: Difficult to sex unless male is in spawning dress. Gravid females with swollen abdomen. The females are often larger than

the males. Description: Fins: D XVII-XIX/7-8, A XVII-XX/11-15, P 9, V 1, C 13. Scales: llr 27-29, dlr 14-16. Captive Care: For best results with the smaller labyrinths it is best to keep them in single pairs. Small aquaria are adequate, but a minimum 20l capacity should be used. Thick planting in the background and free swimming space in the foreground is recommended. Feeding consists of a variety of live and dry foods. The male often spends a long time building and improving his bubble nest. It consists of relatively large bubbles and, if available, will be made under a floating leaf. If built on the bare water surface it is usually unstable. In such cases it can be as much as 40cm in diameter (Vierke). while he has a bubble nest, the male will frequently show his pairing colors. If he sees a gravid female he will swim to her, stand himself diagonally before her, and dance; while doing this he gradually approaches the nest and the

147

Upper left: A male Honey Gourami, *Colisa chuna*. Upper right: A pair of *Colisa chuna* in nuptial maneuvers. Lower photo: The pointed posterior upper tip of the dorsal fin of this male *Colisa chuna* contrasts with the more rounded dorsal tip of the female *C. chuna*.

A beautiful male *Colisa chuna* guarding the eggs in his bubblenest which he built under a leaf floating at the surface of the water.

female will, sometimes haltingly, follow him. After spawning, the eggs are usually concentrated in one part of the nest. The nest is no longer improved or repaired and it often begins to fall apart. However, the eggs are kept in position by water spitting. The male spits water droplets into the air which pull eggs back below the surface as they land. They are then easier to recognize and the male can place them back in the nest. The eggs are about 1mm in diameter. Each spawning act produces about 20 eggs and altogether about 300 are produced. It is recommended that the eggs are separated from the parents after a few hours. The fry hatch in about 24 hours and are free swimming in another three days. Unlike those of other *Colisa* species, the eggs and fry are remarkably dark in color. Special Behavior: The male's courting and guiding procedure is unique to the genus *Colisa* . Catching prey by spitting water has also been observed in this species. Misc: In view of the relative sobriety of color and pattern, this species is not exactly commonly available in the trade.

Colisa fasciata male.

Colisa fasciata

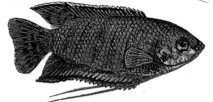

Colisa fasciata (Bloch and Schneider, 1801). Banded Gourami *fasciata* (Lat.) – banded. Other Names in the Literature: *Trichogaster fasciatus* Bloch and Schneider, 1801; *Trichopodus colisa* Hamilton-Buchanan 1822; *T. bejeus* Hamilton-Buchanan 1822; *T. cotra* Hamilton-Buchanan, 1822; *Colisa vulgaris* Cuvier and Valenciennes, 1831; *C. bejeus* Cuvier and Valenciennes, 1831; *C. cotra* Cuvier and Valenciennes, 1831; *C. ponticeriana* Cuvier and Valenciennes, 1831; *Polyacanthus fasciatus* Cuvier and Valenciennes, 1831; *Trichogaster fasciatus* var. Playfair; *T. fasciatus* var. *playfairi* Day, 1878; *Colisa fasciata* Myers, 1923. First Description: Bloch and Schneider (1801): *Systema ichthyol.* p. 164, Plate XXXVI *(Trichogaster fasciatus).* Natural Range: Northern India, Assam. Ecology: Ponds and slow flowing waters. Total Length: Males 100m (after Day, 137mm). Females about 80mm. Sex Determination: The male is larger and more brilliantly colored than the female. The female is gray and has darker bands along the body. A broken line runs from the eye to the tail base. The rear of the dorsal fin is pointed in the male, rounded in the female. Description: Fins: D XIII-XVI/9-14, A XV-XVIII/11-18, P 10-12, V 1, C 15-18. Scales: llr 29-31. Color varies territorially. Captive Care: May be kept in species or community tanks but the former is recommended if breeding is contemplated. The bubble nest can be built without the help of vegetation, but if available, the bubbles will be formed beneath or between floating leaves. The male makes a number of bubbles on the surface then carries them under the nest. About 160 eggs are produced per spawning act and altogether 500-1,000 are laid. The fry hatch in about 24 hours and they are free swimming in another 3 days. Special Behavior: Water droplet spitting in brood care and in catching prey has been observed in this species. Sand hills are also sometimes formed, after the male spits sand into the nest. Misc: Due to the many color variations of

this species, it has sometimes been confused with the closely related *C. labiosa* .

Colisa labiosa

Colisa labiosa (Day, 1878). Thick-lipped Gourami. Other Names in the Literature: *Trichogaster labiosus* Day, 1878; *Colisa labiosa* Myers, 1923. First Description: Day (1878): *Fishes of India*, p. 374, Plate LXXIX, fig. 4 *(Trichogaster labiosus).* Natural Range: Burma; according to Day in the Irrawaddy near Rangoon (probably the Irrawaddy area), Sittang River and Tenasserim. Total Length: After Day, longer than 76mm. Female about 60mm. Sex Determination: Like *C. fasciata,* the sexes are simple to differentiate. Male is more colorful with pointed dorsal fin. Female smaller, less colorful and with rounded dorsal. Female also with dark bands and broken line from eye to tail base. Description: Fins: D XVII-XIX/7-9, A XVII-XX/15-20, P 10-11, V 1, C 15-18. Scales llr 29-31. Captive Care: As described for *C. fasciata* . Misc: Pinter (1960), Stallknecht (1962) and Neupert (1965) were concerned with whether *C. labiosa* was a species in its

152

own right or belonged to *C. fasciata*. Due to cross breedings, it can be certain that a very close relationship exists. Morphological and anatomical points were intensively studied by Neupert, who found some notable differences. To date however, no firm conclusion regarding the status of this fish has been reached. Neupert's initiative in updating the classification of *Colisa* will no doubt bring an eventual conclusion. His research involved a great deal of material, including catches from the exact borders of the appropriate ranges. *C. labiosa* may be crossed with both *C. lalia* and *C. fasciata*.

Colisa lalia

Colisa lalia (Hamilton-Buchanan, 1822). Dwarf Gourami. *lalia* - after the local name in the Ooriah district. Other Names in the Literature: *Trichopodus lalius* Hamilton-Buchanan, 1822; *Colisa lalius* Cuvier and Valenciennes, 1831; *C. unicolor* Cuvier and

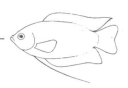

Left: A male Thick-lipped Gourami, *Colisa labiosa.* Below: A male Dwarf Gourami, *Colisa lalia.*

Spawning sequence (eight photos) showing the Thick-lipped Gourami,
Colisa labiosa spawning. The series runs through four photos on the top

of these two pages, from left to right. Thousands of eggs are produced
and they float into the nest which is made of small floating water plants.
155

Spawning sequence of the Dwarf Gourami, *Colisa lalia*. These eight photos run sequentially across the top of the two pages, from left to right. The male uses small plants to build his nest. He entices the

female to join him under the nest, wraps around her body and squeezes the eggs out of her as he fertilizes them at the same time. The lighter than water eggs float right up into the nest with very little assistance from the male.

Valenciennes, 1831; *Trichogaster fasciatus* Guenther, 1861; *T. unicolor* Guenther, 1861; *Colisa lalia* Myers, 1923. First Description: Hamilton-Buchanan (1822): *Fishes Ganges,* pp. 120 and 372 *(Trichopodus lalius).* Natural Range: India, west Bengal and Assam. Areas of the Ganges, Jamuna and Brahmaputra rivers. Ecology: In many kinds of waters; prefers thick vegetation. Often found in paddy fields where it has arrived via irrigation water. Total Length: About 60mm. Sex Determination: Male more colorful and with pointed dorsal pennant. Belly, blue-green. Female light-gray, less colorful and with rounded dorsal. Sex may be determined at first sight. Captive Care: As for preceding species. Unlike other *Colisa* species the male uses a large amount of vegetation in nest building; not only dead material but also fine, feathery leaves torn from the living plants. Peat fibers, roots and large leaves may

also be used in the nest building. Sometimes even whole plants, larger than the fish itself, may be transported to the nest. Each part is meticulously bound together by opercular aeration, which produces tiny, foam-like bubbles. The nest can be up to 10 cm in diameter and 3cm thick. During spawning, any eggs which do not end up directly in the nest are collected by the male and stored away. The eggs are underlaid with fine bubbles. About 60 glass clear eggs are produced per spawning act and altogether about 800 eggs are produced. The fry hatch in about 24 hours and swim freely in another three days. When defending his territory the male becomes very aggressive and will not hesitate to attack fishes even several times larger than himself. Special Behavior: Sometimes the male *C. lalia* will spit grains of sand into the nest which will fall to the substrate and eventually form a sand hill. This behavior is mainly seen when the spawn becomes infected with fungus or after a non-productive spawning. Misc: *C. lalia* is one of the most attractive labyrinth fishes and has almost always been available to the hobbyist. *C. lalia* has been crossed with

This red mutation of *Colisa lalia,* the Dwarf Gourami, is known under various trade names such as The Blushing Gourami, the Red Gourami, etc. The male is shown here constructing his nest. He uses small bubbles to keep the nest afloat.

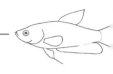

C. *labiosa* (Vierke, 1971 and 1972). All the hybrids developed into phenotypical, sterile males.

Colisa sota

Colisa sota (Hamilton-Buchanan , 1822).Other Names in the Literature: *Trichopodus sota* Hamilton-Buchanan, 1822; *Colisa sota* Cuvier and Valenciennes, 1831; *Trichogaster sota* Regan, 1909. First Description: Hamilton-Buchanan (1822): *Fish. Ganges,* p. 120. Natural Range: Ganges River area. Nine specimens to 45mm total length collected at Deberoo (Day). Total Length: about 45mm. Description (after Regan, 1909): Fins: D XVII-XVIII/7-9, A XII-XX/11-13. Scales: llr 27-29. Brownish with darker flecks along the scale rows. Fins are not marked. Misc: Rarely imported. No conclusion has been reached to date as to whether C. *sota* deserves specific ranking. References and illustrations in the literature give one the impression that this could be female C. *chuna*. Further research in the collection area is required before a definite answer can be found.

160

Subfamily Sphaerichthyinae

Genus *Parasphaerichthys* Prashad and Mukerji, 1929.

Parasphaerichthys ocellatus

Parasphaerichthys ocellatus Prashad and Mukerji, 1929. First Description: Prashad and Mukerji (1929): The fish of the Indawgyi Lake and the streams of the Myitkyina district (Upper Burma). Natural Range: Small, dark waters in the area of the Great Burmese Lakes, Indawgyi, in the north of the country and the river area of the Myitykina district. Living specimens have not yet been imported. It is said to closely resemble *Sphaerichthys osphromenoides* .

A female laden and swollen with eggs. This Chocolate Gourami was spawned by the author for the first time. No one has duplicated this feat yet.

Genus *Sphaerichthys* Canestrini, 1860.
Sphaerichthys (Gr.) spherical fish. Number of Species: 2. Shape: Laterally flattened, slightly elongate to roundish. Fin Formation: long, thread-like ventrals (I/5), 7-13 hard and 7-10 soft dorsal rays, 7-11 hard and 16-22 soft anal rays.

Sphaerichthys acrostoma

Sphaerichthys acrostoma Vierke, 1979. First Description: Vierke (1979): Beschreibung einer neuen Art und einer neuen Unterart aus der Gattung *Sphaerichthys* aus Borneo. *Das Aquarium*, p. 342. Albrecht Philler Verlag, Minden. Natural Range: Mentaya river system, about 250km northwest of Banjarmasin, Kalimantan (south Borneo). Ecology: In a river with a depth of about 80cm. Substrate with a growth of *Cryptocoryne.* The fish were caught in a reedy area. Water was dark-brown colored. Water temperature at the time (March, 1978) was 32° C. Total hardness 0 degrees, carbonate hardness 0.5 degrees, pH 7.6 (Foersch, 1979). Total Length: 68mm. Sex Determination: Male light gray with dark band from eye to mouth. Female somewhat

smaller with more pointed head. Description: Fins: D VI/9, A IX/20, V I/5, C 14. Scales: llr 28 (2 on tail base), dlr 16. Unpaired fins are light-blue bordered. Captive Care: It is recommended that this species is kept in as large a tank as possible. It may be kept in harder water but, for breeding, soft water, filtered through peat is essential. Substrate materials and plants are best not used in the breeding tank. Water temperature should be kept between 25 and 28°C. Feed with mosquito larvae, Daphnia and Cyclops. They will also take fruit flies from the water surface. Like *S. osphromenoides,* this species also spawns on the substrate. To date, no reports of aquarium breeding.

Sphaerichthys osphromenoides selatanensis Vierke, 1979

Sphaerichthys osphromenoides selatanensis Vierke, 1979. First Description: Vierke

(1979): Beschreibung einer neuen Art und einer Unterart aus der Gattung *Sphaerichthys* aus Borneo. *Das Aquarium*, pp. 339-342. Natural Range: Near to Banjarmasin in south east Kalimantan (south Borneo). Ecology: Slow moving, about 1m wide stream with loamy bottom and *Cryptocoryne* growth. Water brown in color but clear. Temperature about 27°C. Total hardness: 0.5 degrees; pH 5. Total Length: 50mm. Sex Determination: Male somewhat darker and slimmer than the female. The dorsal and anal fins are white bordered. When excited those of the male are dark brown to dark gray, while those of the female are reddish. It is difficult to sex young specimens but easy with adults. Description: Fins: D VII/8-9, A VII/21-23, V I/5, C 13. Scales: llr 29-30 (1). Captive Care: As for the nominate form. Misc: It is possible that this subspecies

A typical Chocolate Gourami in poor condition. The fish must be superbly conditioned prior to spawning. They show this with a dark chocolate color.

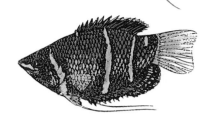

described by Vierke is *S. vaillanti* (described by Pellegrin). As no illustration was available with the original description of the latter, it is not possible to compare. In his description, Vierke mentioned differences in fin formulae and the proportions and form of the caudal.

Sphaerichthys osphromenoides

Sphaerichthys osphromenoides Canestrini, 1860. Chocolate Gourami. *osphromenoides*-gourami-like. Other Names in the literature: *Osphromenus malayanus* Duncker, 1904. First Description: Canestrini (1860): *Verhandl. Zool. Botan. Gesellschaft Vienna, X, p. 707.* Natural Range: Southern part of Malayan Peninsula, Sumatra and Kalimantan. Ecology: Ponds and ditches with extremely mineral-poor water. The water is coffee brown (Reichelt). Water temperature about 30°C, pH 5.5, water hardness 0.5 dH (Schmidt). No water plants. The fish usually hide under overhanging vegetation. Schmidt found this species in sewage-polluted ditches near to human habitations in Palembang (south eastern

Sumatra). The water temperature here was 32°C, with a hardness of 3-5 dH and a pH of 6.5. Total Length: about 63mm. Sex Determination: The male has a pointed dorsal fin; the female's is rounded; however, unless the fins are spread, the difference is difficult to see as these are of similar length in both sexes. Description: Fins: D VIII-XII/7-10, A VII-10/18-22, P 8-10, V I/5, C 13. Scales: llr 26-30, dlr 14-15. Captive Care: With colors resembling those of coral fishes, the Chocolate Gourami, for a long time, was supposed to be a difficult aquarium fish. However, massive imports during the 70s led to the fish being kept in various situations, so that good experiences in their care were soon being reported. The fish seemed to live longest in a large tank with soft water, enriched with humus. Feeding is possible with live or dry food. Mosquito larvae appear to be the favorite food. For breeding, the fish must be kept in soft, acid water. It is

Top, left: Female Chocolate Gourami in breeding condition. Top, right: The same fish showing its bright colors. Bottom: A male Chocolate Gourami, *Sphaerichthys osphromenoides.*

best to use pure water which has been filtered through peat and to add just 1l of tap water per 20l of the peat water. The water temperature can be maintained around 25°C. Successful breedings are however, still a rarity. A gravid female can easily be recognized by the swollen abdomen. She will approach the male time and again. If the male is ready to spawn he will display to her. Both individuals take on dark courtship colors and circle around each other with spread fins. They then seek out a suitable spawning area. At first they will separate frequently and come back together when a suitable spawning site has been found. They swim around each other a few times, near to the substrate. They will continue bouts of displaying and trial pairings for some time. The female bends her body and the male swims into her embrace (sometimes the opposite may occur). The male's tail fin now becomes deep black, and the female inflates her red-colored throat pouch. Both individuals hold their mouths wide open; courtship only stops when the fish need to obtain air. Spawning takes place

relatively quickly. The male swims into the female's embrace and begins to shiver and give out his milt; at the same time, the female releases her cream colored eggs. The 2mm eggs lay on the substrate and the female begins to collect them . About 80 eggs are laid altogether. After the first 20-30 eggs have been collected, the collecting begins to slow down. At first, not all eggs are collected in the female's throat pouch. She swims to the surface to obtain air, making chewing motions with her mouth. The male collects more eggs and brings them to the female, spitting them in front of her mouth and she snaps them up immediately. With her chewing motions, she makes more space for eggs in her throat pouch. When all the eggs are stored away in the throat pouch, one can see a strong swelling of the throat. The female stays near the water surface and obtains air more frequently than usual. The male takes no further interest in the female. The fry, about 5mm long, emerge from the throat pouch in about 14 days. *S. osphromenoides* is therefore a mouth-brooding labyrinth fish.

This historical series of photographs shows the Chocolate Gourami spawning for the first time. The heavy eggs are collected in the mouth of the female where she broods them.

Sphaerichthys Vaillanti

Sphaerichthys vaillanti, Pellegrin, 1930. Other Names in the Literature: *Ctenops nobilis* Vaillant, 1893. Natural Range: Sebroang, Kalimantan (Borneo). Total Length: About 50mm. Description: Fins: D VII-VIII/7-8, A IX-XI/16-18, P 11, V I/5. Scales: llr 27-29.

The photos above and below are typical Chocolate Gouramis from various locations. They are rarely ever found in petshops under ideal conditions, so they can hardly be appreciated for their elegant and serene beauty. They are extremely peaceful with deportment and spawning behavior that is probably the most interesting of any gourami. Top photo by Arend van den Nieuwenhuizen. Bottom photo by Dr. S. Frank.

Family Helostomidae

Genus *Helostoma* Cuvier and Valenciennes, 1831 (in Cuvier, *Le regne animal,* ed. 2, vol. 2, p. 228. *Helostoma* (Gr.) - referring to the large lips. Number of Species: 1. Size: to 300mm. Shape: Laterally flattened, elongate. Fin Formation: Short ventrals (I/5), 16-18 hard and 13-16 soft dorsal rays, 13-15 hard and 17-19 soft anal rays.

Helostoma temminckii

Helostoma temminckii Cuvier and Valenciennes, 1831. Kissing Gourami. *temmincki* - after the Dutch doctor Temminck. Local Names: Several in Thailand including pla ikoh, pla mor tan, pla itan, pla bai tan and pla wi. Other Names in the Literature: *Helostoma temmincki* Cuvier and Valenciennes, 1831; *H. tambakkan* and *H. oligacanthum* Bleeker, 1845; *H. servus* Kaup, 1863; *H. temmincki* Bleeker, 1865; *H. rudolfi* Bellanca, 1968 (for yellow form); *H. xanthoristi* Pinter, 1968 (for yellow form). First Description: Cuvier and Valenciennes (1831): *Hist. Nat Poiss.,* VII, p. 342, plate CXCIV *(Helostoma temmincki).* Natural Range: Thailand, Java, Borneo, Sumatra. Ecology: Slow moving waters; but mainly in ponds, marshes and artificial waters, thick with aquatic vegetation. Total Length: Up to 300mm reported. Largest specimen measured in Thailand was 255mm. In a fish farm in Florida, largest specimen produced was 206mm. Sex Determination: No obvious differences in color or fins. Females can be distinguished when gravid. Description: Fins: D XVI-XVIII/13-15, A XIII-XV/17-19, P 9-11, V I/5, C 13. Scales: llr 43-48. Captive Care: These relatively large fish are best obtained as juveniles about 5cm in length. The tank should be as large as possible and definitely not less than 100l capacity. One should not keep too many fish in the tank. Whether one is keeping young or adult specimens, they should be fed on small food. Microorganisms and dry food may be given. The notable feature of this species is the thick lips. These are fleshy and furnished on the inner surface with fine teeth. These are used to graze on algae and other small particles. As the common name suggests these fish often make kissing motions with their lips, this being display behavior. No special requirements regarding water hardness. At

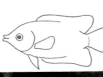

Two forms (above and below) of the Kissing Gourami, *Helostoma temminckii*. There is a grey form and a pink form. Some even are to be found that are much greener, but they are all the same species.

A spawning series of Kissing Gouramis, *Helostoma temminckii*. The male wraps his body about the female and thousands of tiny eggs are released. The eggs float. No nest is usually built.

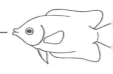

spawning time the female develops a swollen abdomen and both sexes darken in color. The male swims around the female with spread fins but at first she usually drives him off. Then shortly before spawning the female becomes active and pushes the male several times in his belly. The male then swims into a position parallel to the female but facing in the opposite direction. They then beat their tails slowly at first but becoming progressively faster until they end up mouth to mouth. At this stage the kissing starts and continues for some time. Trial pairings will follow in which the male takes the female in a bodily embrace and turns her upside down. Spawning follows with shivering from the male. The eggs are released and float to the water surface where the parent fish take no more notice of them. A bubble nest is not built and spawning takes place anywhere the fish happen to be at the time. Each spawning act produces about 20 eggs at first increasing to 200 later. 10,000 eggs per spawning session is not unusual. The eggs are amber colored at first, darkening in color in about 12 hours. The

172

fry hatch in about 17 hours and are free swimming in another 30 hours. It is best to remove the eggs to a separate rearing tank. The many fry will devour great quantities of microscopic food. Frequent water change and a good diet are essential. Misc: As well as the gray wild form of this species, there is a yellow mutation. It is not clear if this mutation occurs in the wild.

Above: Kissing behavior is not understood by scientists. Facing page: a pair getting ready to spawn.

Family Osphronemidae

Genus *Osphronemus* Lacepede, 1802. *Osphrenome* (Gr.) – to smell or scent (probably a false reference to the function of the labyrinth organ). Number of Species: 1. Size: to 600mm. Shape: Elongate. Fin Formation: Long, thread-like ventrals (I/5), 11-13 hard and 11-13 soft dorsal rays, 9-12 hard and 16-22 soft anal rays.

Osphronemus goramy

Osphronemus goramy Lacepede, 1802. Giant Gourami *goramy* - taken from the native name which is known throughout its natural range (after Rachow). Local Names: According to Smith, in Thailand pla raet (central areas) and pla min (Malayan peninsula). Other Names in the Literature: *Osphroneme goramy* Lacepede, 1802; *Osphromenus olpax* Cuvier, 1817; *O. goramy* Cuvier and Valenciennes, *O. notatus* Cuvier and Valenciennes, 1831; *Osphronemus satyrus,* Bleeker, 1845; *Osphromenus gourami* Regan, 1909. First Description: Lacepede, B.G.E. (1802): *Histoire naturelle des poissons,* vol.3, p. 117 *(Osphroneme goramy).* Natural Range: According to
174

Rachow, originally in Java, possibly Sumatra, Borneo and other islands in the archipelago. In recent times it has extended its range throughout Southeast Asia. Ecology: Ponds, rivers, larger streams, and canals in areas

thickly vegetated with reeds and water plants. The water quality in the various areas in which this species is found varies greatly. It has even been found in brackish water. Total Length: Native fishermen have reported 600mm. Vierke (1978) suggests even 700mm. An authentic record, recorded by Smith (1945), gives a length of 560mm for a specimen caught in 1924. Specimens with a length of more than 400mm are scarce in captivity. Sex Determination: Male: dorsal and anal fins run out to

Above: A young specimen of the Giant Gourami, *Osphronemus goramy*. Below: A group of fully grown Giant Gourami.

a point; large forehead.
Female: dorsal and anal fins
rounded. Description: Fins: D
XI -XIII/11-13, A IX-XII 16-22, V
I/5, C 12-13. Scales: llr 30-35.
Captive Care: Only young
specimens are usually suitable
for the home aquarium as,
with a good diet, they soon
outgrow their tank. They are
not very choosy regarding
their food and will eat
waterplants, lettuce, fruit and
rice, as well as cooked meat,
daphnia, tubifex and mosquito
larvae. Even bread, boiled
potatoes and other vegetables
176

A 4 inch long young Giant Gourami.

The rasping teeth of a Giant
Gourami indicate it is equipped for
rasping algae from wood and
stones. Photo by Dr. Herbert R.
Axelrod at Berlin Aquarium,
Germany.

are greedily devoured. In its native habitat, it has therefore been designated water hog. Being the largest of all labyrinth fishes it really belongs in large, public aquaria. As it eats a great deal, and has an appropriate metabolic rate, frequent water changes are necessary. In the public aquarium this is accomplished by water circulatory sytems. No special requirements regarding water hardness and the water

178

Dr. Herbert R. Axelrod on his famous Gourami Expedition (1972) when he used a native lift net to catch gouramis. He would set the net in the water and have a native boy drop bits of food into the net every few minutes until several fishes appeared. Then he would lift the net as the fish came to eat and capture them. This photo was taken in Indonesia. On the facing page is a typical habitat of a Giant Gourami. Axelrod caught a dozen Giant Gouramis here in Indonesia.

temperature should be maintained in the region of 24°. According to Deraniyagala, the fish are sexually mature at 6 months and, with optimal rearing, about 120mm in length. Breeding in the home aquarium has probably not been accomplished. Various conflicting reports have been given regarding the breeding behavior of this species. In one case, the fish are supposed to build a bubble nest near to the bank and to spawn under it. According to Bhimachar, David and Muniappa (1944) however (taken from observations at a fish farm), the fish build an almost spherical nest using pieces of reeds. These nests are about 40cm in diameter and 30cm deep but vary from one to another. The entrance to the nest is circular and about 10cm in diameter; it always points in the direction of the deepest part of the pond. The nest is anchored to the reed stems, about 15-25cm below the water surface, and 30cm above the substrate. The male takes 8-10 days to build the nest. The fish spawn throughout most of the year, while nests are mostly built in April and May.

Spawning has not been observed, but it is suspected that it takes place outside the nest and that the male then carries the eggs to the nest. The eggs are covered with further pieces of vegetation. On 20th May 1943 a nest was found to contain 1450 newly hatched fry. Kulkani (1939) reports 2-3,000 fry in a nest. The eggs are slightly oval in form, transparent yellow in color and about 2.7 - 2.9mm in diameter. The fry hatch in about 40 hours. The male is said to guard the offspring for about 14 days after the spawning. Misc: Lacepede's first description of this species was based on a manuscript by Commerson which used the name *Osphronemus olfax*. During growth, the fish change their appearance. While juveniles have a pointed head and a flat snout, adult specimens show a swollen forehead, thick lips and chin. The swollen head is particularly prominent in the male. The color also changes. Juveniles are brownish, with dark cross-bands and an eye spot on the lower tail base. Older specimens are usually gray, the back dark with the head and underside much lighter. When excited, the fins

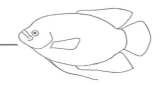

turn dark gray. In its present range, which includes even Australia, South America (Cayenne, French Guiana) South Africa, Egypt and Algeria, it is regarded as an excellent food fish and, in some places, it is cultivated. Only juvenile specimens are usually available through the aquarium trade.

Dr. Axelrod collected this wild Giant Gourami in Indonesia. It measured about 20 inches long and made a giant meal for Axelrod and his native helper. Photo by Dr. Herbert R. Axelrod.

Dr. Axelrod recognizes three different body shapes. The shallow form is illustrated on the previous page. The medium depth form is shown above and the deep-bodied forms which he photographed in Berlin in 1977 is shown below. No one has seriously studied this economically valuable fish in many decades.

Family Anabantidae

Subfamily Anabantinae
This subfamily comes in two geographically separated ranges.

Southeast Asian Range
Genus *Anabas* Cuvier and Cloquet, 1816. *Anabas* (Gr.) – climber. Number of Species: 1. Size: to 250mm. Shape: Round in section, elongate. Fin Formation: Short ventrals (I/5), 16-19 hard and 16-19 soft dorsal rays, 9-11 hard and 8-11 soft anal rays.

The black "moustache" of *Anabas* helps distinguish it from similar *Ctenopoma* species.

Anabas testudineus

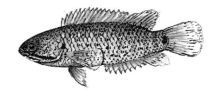

Anabas testudineus (Bloch, 1792). Climbing Perch. *testudineus* (Lat.) – turtle-like. Local Names: In Thailand mainly pla mor, in the area of Bangkok pla mor thai; in north Thailand and Laos, pla sadat. Other Names in the Literature: *Anthias testudineus* Bloch, 1792; *Perca scandens* de Daldorff, 1797; *Amphiprion testudineus* Bloch and Schneider, 1801; *A. scansor* Bloch and Schneider, 1801;

Lutianus testudo Lacepede, 1803; *L. scandens* Lacepede, 1803; *Sparus testudineus* Shaw 1803; *S. scandens* Shaw, 1803; *Cojus cobojius* Hamilton-Buchanan, 1822; *Anabas scandens* Cuvier and Valenciennes, 1831; *A. spinosus* Gray, 1834; *A. variegatus* Bleeker, 1851; *A. macrocephalus* Bleeker, 1854; *A. oligolepis* Bleeker, 1855; *A. microcephalus* Bleeker, 1857; *A. trifoliatus* Kaup, 1860; *A. elongatus* Reuvens. First Description: Bloch (1792): *Naturgeschichte des auslaendischen Fische,* VI, p 121, plate CCCXXII *(Anthias testudineus).* Natural Range: After Smith: Southern China, Vietnam, Thailand, Malaysia, Burma, India, Sri Lanka, the

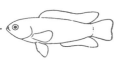

Earl Kennedy of the Philippine Islands photographed these beautiful golden forms of *Anabas testudineus,* the Climbing Perch .

A pond near Korat about 85 miles northwest of Bangkok, Thailand. This pond contained *Trichogaster trichopterus, Betta splendens* and *Anabas testudineus.*

Philippines and Indonesia. Ecology: All kinds of fresh waters, including large rivers; but mostly in canals, ditches, lakes, ponds and swamps. Total Length: to 250mm, but to 160mm in the aquarium. Sex Determination: Easy to distinguish in adults. The male is slimmer than the female, which is plump in the abdomen. Description: Fins: D XVI-XIX/7-10, A IX-XI/8-11, P 13, C 13. Scales: llr 26-31. Captive Care: One must take into consideration the size and predatory habit of this fish before deciding to keep it. An aquarium of 100l minimum

Above: A school of *Anabas testudineus* photographed by Dr. Herbert R. Axelrod at the Berlin (Germany) aquarium.

Facing page, top: A 6 inch specimen of the Climbing Perch, *Anabas testudineus*. Facing page, bottom: A young 3 inch specimen of *Anabas testudineus*.

capacity is required. A space at least 10 cm wide between the water surface and the aquarium lid must be left as this species often jumps right out of the water to obtain air. There are no special requirements regarding the water hardness. The tank should be thickly planted except for a small area in the foreground where the fish can display and spawn. It is best to keep these fish in single pairs as they can be very aggressive. Food can consist of all the usual live and dry foods. It is useful also to feed them the young of livebearers. With good feeding and frequent water changes the

female will soon become noticeably gravid. The fish spawn without any preparations (no bubble nest is built); usually on the substrate or in midwater. The pair goes into an embrace and the spawning products are produced. The eggs are glass clear and float to the surface. About 200 eggs per spawning act are produced - altogether up to 5,000. They are about 0.6mm in diameter. The parents pay no further attention to the eggs; it is best to remove them to a rearing tank. At 24°C, the eggs will hatch in about 23 hours. The tiny fry are just 2-3mm long. In 2 days, they are free swimming and must be fed with microscopic organisms. In another 5 days they reach 7mm and should be about 16mm at one month. Special Behavior: As its common name implies, the Climbing Perch possesses the facility to move out of the water. This usually occurs only in damp areas; they use the pectoral fins, the gill covers and the tail to walk. During heavy rainfall, or in the early hours, they may be seen wandering in groups from one water to the next. Their climbing talents pose some problems when catching them up. If a large-meshed net

is used, they will get their hard fin rays entangled and the net will be damaged; if a fine-meshed net is used, they will simply climb out; so beware ! This species is mainly night-active and also spawns at night. Misc: Not imported very often, this species is perhaps more suited for the labyrinth specialist. It is often seen in public aquaria and zoological collections.

African Range

Two genera of labyrinth fishes are found in Africa. A third genus *(Oshimia)* has been described, but only one specimen *(O. marchei)* has been found. The status of this genus/species requires further research. However, for completeness, this species is included at the end of this section.

Genus *Sandelia* Castenau, 1861. Number of Species: 2. Size: 140-180mm. Shape: Round in section, elongate. Fin Formation: Short ventrals, 12-17 hard and 8-10 soft dorsal rays, 6-8 hard and 8-11 soft anal rays.

Top: Typical habitat of *Anabas*. Bottom left: The Cape Bush Fish, *Sandelia capensis*. Bottom right: *Sandelia bainsii* which as yet has no common name because it is so rarely seen in the aquarium.

189

Sandelia bainsii

Sandelia bainsii Castenau, 1861 Other Names in the Literature: *Sandelia bainsii* Castenau, 1861; *Ctenopoma microlepidotum* Guenther, 1861; *Spirobranchus bainsii* Boulenger, 1905. First Description: Castenau (1861): *Mem. Poiss. Afr. Austr., p. 37 (Sandelia bainsii).* Natural Range: South coastal areas of Africa. Description: Fins: D XV-XVII/9-10, A VII-VIII/9-10. Scales: llr 33-35, dlr 16-17/14-15. Captive Care: There are no details available, but probably similar to that described for *Anabas testudineus.*

Sandelia capensis

Sandelia capensis Cuvier and Valenciennes, 1831 Cape Bush Fish, Cape Perch, Cape Kurper. Other Names in the

Literature: *Spirobranchus capensis* Cuvier and Valenciennes, 1831; *Anabas capensis* Cuvier and Valenciennes, 1831. First Description: Cuvier and Valenciennes (1831): *Hist. Poiss., VII, p. 392, pl. CC. (Spirobranchus capensis).* Natural Range: South Africa including the Langevlei, Elands, Camtoos, Coega and Couritz rivers. Total Length: after Boulenger, 140mm; Jacobi, 210mm. Sex Determination: No details known. Description: D XII-XIV/8-10, A VI-VII/8-11. Scales: llr 27-30, dlr 14-18/6-12. Captive Care: No details available. Probably as for *Anabas testudineus.* Special Behavior: Male and female are sexually mature within one year. The smallest sexually mature female examined by Jacobi was only 5cm. They spawn in still water areas near to the substrate. A short bodily embrace takes place and the eggs sink to the bottom where they adhere to surfaces. The eggs are guarded by the male. No bubble nest is made. Misc: Harrison (1952) reported that specimens which had been out of the water for several hours (!!) in the African summer, appearing dried up

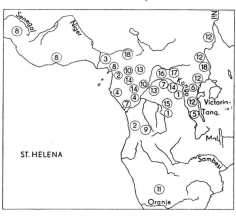

and lifeless, recovered when returned to the water. Liem (1952) showed that the genus *Sandelia* developed from the genus *Ctenopoma* and has a simplified labyrinth organ.

Genus *Ctenopoma* Peters, 1844. ktenos (Gr.) – comb lid (from the comb like edge to the gill cover). Number of Species: Not currently clear. Size: 75-200mm. Shape: Variable, from round body section and elongate, to laterally flattened and barely elongate. Fin Formation: short ventrals (I/5), 10-20 hard and 6-12 soft dorsal rays, 7-12 hard and 6-12 soft anal rays. Due to two notable factors, namely different breeding behavior and different external sexual differences, it is likely that a split in the genus will take place. Until this reorganization of the genus occurs, the species are here listed alphabetically in the genus *Ctenopoma*.

1 *C. acutirostre*	10 *C. maculatum*
2 *C. ansorgii*	11 *C. multispinnis*
3 *C. argentoventer*	12 *C. muriei*
4 *C. congicum*	13 *C. nanum*
5 *C. ctenotis*	14 *C. nigropannosum*
6 *C. damasi*	15 *C. ocellatum*
7 *C. fasciolatum*	17 *C. pellegrini*
8 *C. kingsleyae*	16 *C. oxyrhynchum*
9 *C. machadoi*	18 *C. petherici*

ST. HELENA

Ctenopoma   acutirostre

Ctenopoma acutirostre, Pellegrin, 1899. Leopard Ctenopoma, Spotted Climbing Perch. *acutirostre* (Lat.) – pointed snout. Other Names in the Literature: *Ctenopoma*

petherici (not Guenther) Schilthuis, 1891; *C. acutirostre* Pellegrin, 1899; *C. denticulatum* Pellegrin, 1899; *Anabas weeksii* Boulenger, 1905; *A. ocellatus* Boulenger, 1905. First Description: Pellegrin (1899): *Bull. Mus. Paris,* p. 360 *(Ctenopoma acutirostre).* Natural Range: Congo basin: Stanley Pool, Stanley Falls, River Sankuru near Kondue, Kaisa Province. Total Length: to 200mm; in the aquarium rarely over 150mm. Sex Determination: A sure method of sexing is only by examining the spines just behind the eye and on the tail

191

base. The males have well developed spines; the females, even in older specimens, never so well developed. This method can only be carried out, out of water, with a strong lens. Description: Fins: D XIV-XVII/9-12, A IX-X/10-12, P 14, V I/5, C 14. Scales: llr 26-28. Captive Care: Due to the size of this species a tank of minimum 100l is required. More than 2-3 specimens should not be kept together. *C. acutirostre* is nocturnal and requires a well planted tank with plenty of hiding places. Each individual has its own home, where it lurks waiting

Ctenopoma acutirostre. Photo by Dr. Herbert R. Axelrod.

for prey. If a suitably sized fish swims near to its snout, it will be violently sucked up! It will only actively pursue prey when it is extremely hungry. The prey is only snapped up when it is directly in front of the mouth. In general, this species is very shy. They may lose a little of the shyness if kept in a very large aquarium with adequate hiding places. As soon as they are settled in and know the source of food, they will swim slowly to the front glass at feeding time. In a community tank only fish of adequate size should be kept with this species, bearing in mind that it is capable of swallowing a full-grown female guppy. They are however fairly peaceful towards their own species. When each fish has its own regular hiding place, it will stay there all day, almost motionless. Towards evening they become active. Should they meet each other then, they will swim around each other and display, often bombarding each other with water currents by waggling the body. Sometimes they face each other with wide-open mouths, even butting each other with open mouth in the sides. However, they never seem to injure each other during these encounters. They may be kept in almost all kinds of tapwater, at a temperature of 20-24°C. If the fish are to be moved, it is essential to use a fine-meshed net; if a large-meshed net is used, the fish will become entangled in the mesh with their gill spines and very difficult to remove. The fish may be fed on Daphnia, mosquito larvae, meal worms, dragonfly larvae and other large insect larvae. If small fish are given at first, it will be difficult to persuade them to take other food later. Captive breeding has, so far, not been reported. Special Behavior: With this species, one can often observe that the mouth is opened wide for no apparent reason. One can assume that this is yawning! Misc: Large, older specimens tend to lose their spots and show a brownish color over the whole body. Juveniles are almost totally yellowish-white in ground color, this darkening gradually with age.

Ctenopoma acutirostre.

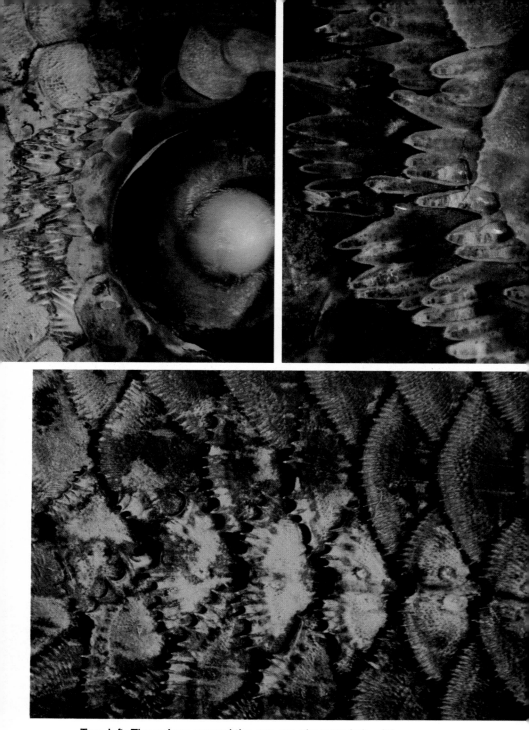

Top, left: The spines around the eye are characteristic of the egg-scattering *Ctenopoma* species. Top, right: A closeup of the spines around the eye. Males have longer and more pronounced spines. Bottom: A closeup of the spiney scales found on the caudal peduncle.

Ctenopoma ansorgii

Ctenopoma ansorgii
(Boulenger, 1912). Ornate
Ctenopoma. *ansorgii* - after
Ansorge, the discoverer of the
species. Other Names in the

Ctenopoma ansorgii.

Literature: *Anabas ansorgii*
Boulenger, 1912. First
Description: Boulenger (1912):
Ann. Mus. Congo. Zool., vol. 2,
p. 23 *(Anabas ansorgii).*
Natural Range: After
Boulenger: Luali River, near
Lundo. Linke found it in the
Camaroons, in the Kienke-
Lobe river system between

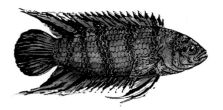

Kribi and Ebulowa, as well as
in a tributary of the Ntema
River. Ecology: In the bank
regions of slow-flowing
waters, where they hide under
roots and overhanging
vegetation near to the bottom.
Such waters are mineral-poor
and have a pH of about 5.
Total Length: Males 80mm,
females 70mm. Description:
Fins: D XVII-XVIII/7, A X-XI/7,
P 7, v I/5, C 12. Scales: llr 28-
30, dlr 2-8/0-5. Captive Care:
This species may be kept in a
community tank, but they
spend most of the day in
195

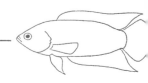

hiding. It is therefore better to keep them in a species tank with a minimum 50l capacity. It may be thinly planted with *Bolbitis heudelotti* and there should be a few good hiding places provided. Bogwood may be used for this. Frequent water changing is important. Tap water is suitable and the temperature should be maintained around 23°C. A filter pump may be used to promote a slow water flow. For breeding, soft, mineral-poor water should be used with a pH around 6. It has proven beneficial to filter the water through peat. May be fed with the usual live foods but seems to prefer mosquito larvae. Floating plants on the water surface will cut down the light intensity and provide sites for the bubble nest. Gravid females are instantly recognizable from their swollen bellies. The male displays to the female with spread fins but he only begins to build the bubble nest a few days later. The nest is built with large bubbles under the leaf of a floating plant. The female swims more and more often to her partner under the nest but is at first driven off. Only when the male is ready, will he, with spread fins,

receive the female under the nest. He will waggle his whole body and the female prods him in the side before they begin to swim around each other. The male bends his body and the female then swims into his embrace. This usually takes place under the bubble nest but now and again may occur on the substrate. With a light shivering, they release the spawning products. The glass clear eggs float slowly to the surface. After spawning, the female pulls back while the male collects the eggs. Shortly after the fish spawn again. Each spawning act produces about 30 eggs - altogether about 600. The fry hatch in about 24 hours. They are free swimming in another 3 days. At 10mm in length, the juveniles already show the beautiful orange coloration and display with spread fins. Adults do not always show the orange color and usually stay sombrely colored in their hiding places. In excitement, the body, with the exception of the belly, becomes greenish and the fins show orange with dark stripes. The tail fin is then smoky-black. The extended, white, soft fin-rays of the male are particularly notable.

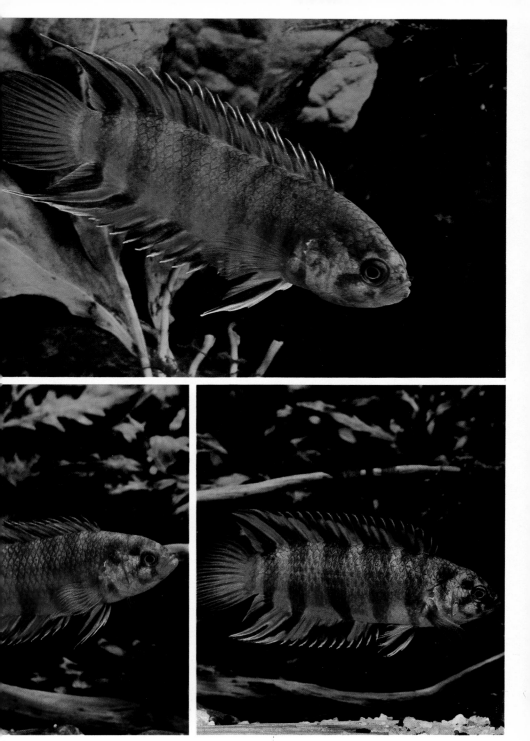

Above: The ornate Ctenopoma, *Ctenopoma ansorgii* in its normal aquarium color. Below: These two photos show the male in his mating or courting colors.

197

Spawning rituals of the Ornate Ctenopoma, *C. ansorgii.* Top: The male colors blaze! This entices the female to butt him in the side. Center: The male spreads his fins and the female takes her position in the U-shape of his body. Bottom: The male embraces the female squeezing clear eggs which float up into the nest under which they spawn.

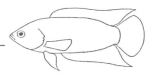

Ctenopoma argentoventer

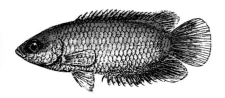

Ctenopoma argentoventer (Ahl, 1922). Dusky Ctenopoma, Silver-bellied Climbing Perch. *argentoventer* (Lat.) – silver-bellied. Other Names in the Literature: *Anabas* spec. Arnold, 1912; *A. africanus* Vetterlein, 1914; *A. argentoventer* Ahl, 1922; *Ctenopoma argentoventer* Myers, 1924; *Anabas (Ctenopoma) peterici* (not *C. petherici* Guenther, 1864) Bruening, 1930. First Description: Ahl (1922): Blaetter fuer Aquarien- und *Terrarienkuende.*, Magdeburg, p. 265 *(Anabas argentoventer).* Natural Range: After Ahel: River basin of the Niger. Total Length: After Rachow: about 150mm. Sex Determination: According to Rachow, only juvenile to half grown specimens show obvious sex differences. This does not agree with other observations on the African bush fishes and can be disputed. However, the sexes may be determined by examining the spines (see *C.*

acutirostre). According to Rachow, pairing takes place in free water. Description: Fins: D XVI/10, A IX/10. Scales: llr 26 Captive Care: As described for *C. acutirostre.* There is no brood care. The eggs float to the surface. The fry hatch in 24 hours and are free swimming in another 3 days.

Ctenopoma congicum

Ctenopoma congicum Boulenger, 1887. Congo Ctenopoma, Congo Climbing Perch. Other Names in the Literature: *Anabas congicus* Boulenger, 1889. First Description: Boulenger (1887): *Ann. Mag. Nat. Hist.,* (5) XIX., p. 148 *(Ctenopoma congicum).* Natural range: Gaboon, Congo: Ogowe, Lower Congo and Ubangi (Hans and Ansorge). Total Length: after Boulenger: 85mm. Sex Determination: Male with larger and pennanted fins. Female with rounded fins and more sombrely colored. Description: Fins: D XVI-XVII/8-9, A IX-XI/9-11. Scales llr 26-28. dlr 13-16/7-11 Captive Care: As for *C. ansorgii* .

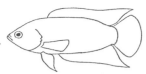

Ctenopoma ctenotis

Ctenopoma ctenotis, (Boulenger, 1920). First Description: Boulenger (1920): On some new fishes from near the west coast of Lake Tanganyika. *Proc. Zool. Soc. London,* p. 399. Natural Range: West Zaire, Zambia, Malawi. River near to the west coast of Lake Tanganyika. No further information is available on this species.

Ctenopoma damasi

Ctenopoma damasi (Poll, 1939). Pearl Ctenopoma, Damas Climbing Perch. Other Names in the Literature: *Anabas damasi* Poll, 1939. First Description: Poll (1939): Poissons in Exploration du Parc National Albert, Mission H. Damas (1935-1936): *Inst des Parcs Nationaux du Congo Belg. Fasc.,* (Bruxelles), 1-73. *(Anabas damasi).* Natural Range: Congo and Uganda around Lake Edward (Greenwood, 1958). Poll (1939) on the Congo side and Berns and Peters (1969) on the Ugandan side confirmed. Ecology: Papyrus swamps on the southern edge of the Kazinga Canal. In small swamp pools with oxygen poor water. Many specimens were also found in a pond which was overgrown with *Pistia.* A few *C. muriei* were also found here. The fish usually hide among the weeds near the bank and avoid the open water. Total length: Moerike (1977) reports: males to 72mm, females to 61mm. Sex Determination: Males about 1cm longer than females and darker colored. During the breeding season the male colors matt blue-black which appears metallic when he is under the nest or in the process of courtship or spawning. Description: Fins: D XIV-XIX/6-9, A IX-XII/6-9. Scales: llr 26-30, dlr 13-19/8-13. Captive Care: This species requires plenty of hiding places in the aquarium. They also like to lurk under floating plants, especially if they can conceal themselves between the leaves. In a community tank, these fish are hardly ever seen. It is therefore better to keep them in a species tank with perhaps 1 or 2 pairs. A tank approx. 70x30x30 is adequate. No special requirements regarding water quality. Water temperature

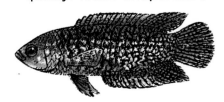

Top: The Pearl Ctenopoma, *Ctenopoma damasi*. Bottom left: The Bullseye Ctenopoma, *C. ocellatum*. Bottom, right: A young female *Ctenopoma congicum*.

Ctenopoma congicum collected and photographed in the Congo by Dr. Herbert R. Axelrod. It is very similar to the *Ctenopoma fasciolatum* shown below except the spots in the fins are pigmented in *congicum* and clear in *fasciolatum,* and the pelvic fins are much longer in congicum. Lower photo by Kresmser.

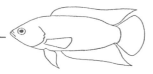

around 20-25°C. Feed on a variety of live and dry foods. The fish are not very active during the day and usually swim only to obtain air at the surface. However, they become very active during spawning time. This occurs first when the fish are about 8 months of age. It is best to provide soft mineral poor water at this time. The female can be seen to be gravid by her swollen belly. The male begins to build a bubble nest which may be free on the water surface or among floating plants or leaves. A free floating nest is usually about 10cm across and 0.5cm thick, while one built under a plant is usually only about 4cm across and 1.5cm thick. It takes hours, sometimes days for the nest to be built to the male's satisfaction. The male works ever harder and becomes darker. The female takes on a light spawning color and tries to approach the bubble nest but at first the male drives her off. If she manages to get under the nest and give the male a light prod

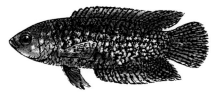

in the side, he will change his attitude, display and then take her in a spawning embrace. After shivering movements, the spawning products are released. The eggs float slowly to the surface. The embrace lasts about 30 seconds. The wife releases herself first and swims quickly to her hiding place. If not she is viciously driven off by the male   who then works further on the nest. After 10-20 minutes, the female returns and another spawning act takes place; the intervals between the spawning acts become progressively less. Altogether, spawning takes 2-3 hours and 300-1200 eggs are produced, averaging 0.76mm in diameter (Moerike, 1977). At 27°C, the fry hatch in 26-31 hours and are about 2mm long. At 4 days they become free swimming and must receive nourishment. Special Behavior: If several pairs are kept, it can happen that females will change partners during spawning. Misc: The young fish first take in atmospheric air at an age of 37-45 days. They are then about 7.7mm long. *C. damasi* is seldom seen in the aquarium and due to its shy behavior is unlikely to increase much in popularity.

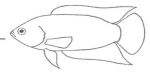

Ctenopoma fasciolatum

Ctenopoma fasciolatum (Boulenger, 1899). Banded Ctenopoma, Banded Climbing Perch. Other Names in the Literature: *Anabas fasciolatus* Boulenger, 1899; *Ctenopoma fasciolatus* Myers, 1924; *C. fasciolatum* Myers, 1926. First Description: Boulenger (1899): Description of a new Osphromenoid Fish from the Congo. *Ann Mag. Nat. Hist.,* (7) III, p. 242 *(Anabas fasciolatus).* Natural Range: Congo region: Monsembe (Upper Congo), Boma (Lower Congo) (after Weeks and Arnold). Ecology: Clear waters

with thickly vegetated banks. Total Length: Males about 85mm, females to 70mm. Sex Determination: Male larger and more intensively colored than the female; also with larger fins. The ends of the dorsal and anal fins run out to a point in the male. This is not so in the female. Gravid females are brownish, with a light stripe extending from behind the gill cover to the tail base. The male's ventrals are longer than those of the female and blue colored. Depending on the area of capture some males show more blue, others more brown on the body (in the latter case, the blue is only obvious on the anal fins). Description: D XVI/9-11, A X/9-11, C 12. Scales: llr 27-28, dlr 14-15/9-11.

Captive Care: This species may be kept just as easily in a community aquarium as in a species tank. There are no special requirements regarding water quality. Unlike the preceding species, *C. fasciolatum* is not too shy and will show itself more frequently in the open areas, but still prefers to spend most of its time among the plants. It may be fed on a variety of live and dry foods. No special water requirements, even for spawning, but floating plants should be available. Temperature should be maintained between 20 and 24°C. The gravid female shows a swollen and light-colored belly as well as a light-colored longitudinal stripe. The male builds a relatively large bubble nest. If no floating plants are available, this may be as much as 20cm in diameter but as

Top: Normal color *Ctenopoma fasciolatum.* The lower photo shows the blue form.

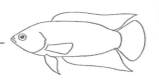

this usually consists of just a thin layer of bubbles, it will soon fall apart when the aquarium lid is removed. Under plants, the nest is about 5cm in diameter and 2cm thick. The bubbles will actually push the waterplant above the water surface. The male now displays his spread fins and blue color more often. If the female comes near, she is brutally driven off. Later the female will make more stormy attempts to reach the nest and, when she manages to prod the male in his body, he becomes peaceful. They swim around each other, then merge into a bodily embrace; the female is gripped by the male's body and usually held so that her head points diagonally towards the surface. After a light shivering motion, sperm and eggs are produced. The glass clear eggs float slowly to the surface. After spawning, the female goes into hiding, otherwise she will be driven off by the male. Altogether about 1,000 eggs are produced. At 22°C, the fry hatch in 40-48 hours. For best results, the eggs should be removed to a rearing tank. Special Behavior: The fish may spawn daily for some time, but numbers of eggs will

decrease. Brooding males are very aggressive towards all other fish. Other males approaching the bubble nest may be so viciously attacked as to have their fins damaged.

Ctenopoma kingsleyae

Ctenopoma kingsleyae Guenther, 1896. Tail-spot Ctenopoma. *kingsleyae* - after the collector Kingsley. Other Names in the Literature: *Ctenopoma petherici* Guenther, 1867; *Anabas kingsleyae* Boulenger, 1899; *Ctenopoma kingsleyi* Pinter, 1957. First Description: Guenther (1867): *Ann. Mag. Nat. Hist.,* (3), vol. 20, p. 110 (*Ctenopoma petherici*). (1896): *Ann. Mag. Nat. Hist.,* vol. 17, p. 270. Natural Range: Senegal to Congo region. Total Length: Boulenger: 190mm; Ostermoeller: 200mm. Sex Determination: Male has a wide border to the ends of the soft rays of the dorsal and anal fins; this is absent in the female. Sexing is also possible by examination of the spines. Gravid females show a swollen belly. Description: Fins: D XVI-XVIII/8-10, A IX-X/9-11. Scales: llr 25-29, dlr 15-16/8-14. Captive Care: *Ctenopoma*

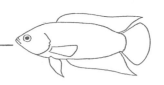

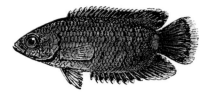

kingsleyae should only be kept in a very large tank as it can reach a large size. In a tank of over 100l capacity, only fish over 5cm in length should be kept in community. Smaller fish will be regarded as prey. If kept on its own, this species is very shy, but if kept in community with other fish, it loses its shyness and will show itself more often. It is best to thickly plant the background of the tank and to leave a relatively large swimming area in the foreground. A particular water quality is not required. The water temperature can be maintained between 22 and 25°C. All manner of live and dry foods can be given, as well as small fish and mealworms. In general, this species is peaceful in a large tank and

Ctenopoma kingsleyae, probably.

occasional encounters do not result in injuries. The species was bred by Ostermoeller. The 18-20cm long fish were placed in a tank 80x40x60cm. Display consisted of a form of nodding. The fish stay parallel to each other, the male with his head somewhat in front of the female's. The male then drops his head about 3mm and floats backwards. This is repeated 3-6 times and the female then copies the action; sometimes croaking tones are said to be heard during this action. During the display, the fish take on a dark gray color, merging into silvery-white on the belly. After the nodding the female prods the male's tail spot. The male strokes the female along the flanks with his open mouth. Finally, they swim to the water surface and entwine lightning fast. Each spawning act produces up to 1,000 eggs; about 20,000 altogether. The parents show no further concern for the floating eggs other than as items for the menu so they should be removed to a rearing tank. The spines seem to play a special role in the spawning process; the male uses them to obtain a better grip on the female. At 23°C, the 2mm long fry hatch in about 48 hours; 24 hours at 24°C. In a further 2-4 days

they are free swimming and about 4mm in length. After 5 months, they will have grown to 5cm. The juvenile fish have an obvious, light border round spot on the tail base. Successful breeding of this species seems to revolve around the age of the fish. Ostermoeller's breeding fish were 6 years old. Misc: Some examples of *C. kingsleyae* have reached the age of 14 years in the aquarium. Larger specimens in excess of 150mm are perhaps better suited to the show tanks of large public aquaria, rather than the home aquarium.

Ctenopoma maculatum

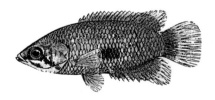

Ctenopoma maculatum Thominot, 1886 Single Spot Ctenopoma. *maculatum* (Lat.) – spotted. Other Names in the Literature: *Ctenopoma maculata* Thominot, 1886; *C. multifasciata* Thominot, 1886; *C. weeksii* Boulenger, 1896; *Anabas weeksii* Boulenger, 1899; *A. pleurostigma* Boulenger, 1903; *A. oxyrhynchus* (not Boulenger);

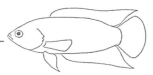

Ctenopoma maculatum, the Single Spot Ctenopoma.

Steindachner, 1913. First Description: Thominot (1886): *Bull. Soc. Philom.*, (7) X., p. 158. Natural Range: Southern Cameroons to the Congo, in the area of Kribi, in the Nten River near Bitoto and Maan. Ecology: Near to the banks of slow moving rivers; under overhanging vegetation and roots. The waters are very mineral-poor, very soft and have a pH value of about 5. Total Length: After Boulenger: 200mm (mostly 90mm in the aquarium). Sex Determination: Reliable sexing is only possible by examining the spines; gravid females have swollen bellies. Description: Fins: D XIV-XVI/9-11, A VII-IX/9-11, C 13. Scales: llr 26-29, dlr 14-19/9-13. Captive Care: The

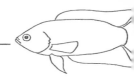

most obvious external feature is the dark spot in the middle of the body. Should be kept as described for *C. acutirostre.* No breeding information is available at the present time. Misc: Very rarely imported. Those fish kept in optimum conditions show a body pattern similar to that of *C. ocellatum* . In addition, the fish show a similarity to *C. oxyrhynchum*, especially older specimens with their uniform brown color and the dark body spot.

Ctenopoma multispinnis

Ctenopoma multispinnis Peters, 1844. Many-spined Ctenopoma. *multispinnis* (Lat.) – many-spined. Other Names in the Literature: *Anabas scandans* (not Daldorff) Bianconi, 1858; *Spirobranchus smithii* Bianconi, 1859; *Ctenopoma multispine* Guenther, 1861; *C. multispinis* Mueller, 1905; *Anabas multispinis* Boulenger, 1905; *Spirobranchus multispines* Woosnam, 1910. First Description: Peters (1844): *Monber. Ak. Berlin,* p. 34. Natural Range: Okorango River (tributary of Lake Ngami in Bechuanaland/Mozambique), Umsitu River in north west

Rhodesia (Zimbabwe), the Zambezi basin. Total Length: about 160mm. Sex Determination: Only possible by examination of the spines. Females heavier when gravid. Description: Fins: D XVII-XVIII/8-9, A VIII-X/8-9. Scales: llr 31-35. Captive Care: As for *C. kingsleyae.* Misc: In a short paper (Parental care in an African fish), Boulenger (1911), reported that on examining a 120mm long female *C. multispinis* he found eggs in a cavity under the gills. It was therefore surmised that this species is a mouthbrooder. However, Peters suggested that these eggs were in fact cysts of the parasite Myxobolus spec.

Ctenopoma muriei

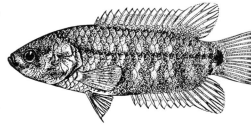

Ctenopoma muriei (Boulenger, 1906). Nile

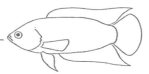

Ctenopoma. Other Names in the Literature: *C. petherici* Guenther, 1864; *Anabas petherici* Pellegrini, 1905; *Anabas muriei* Boulenger, 1906; *A. huoyi* Ahl, 1927. First Description: Boulenger (1906): *Ann. Mag. Nat. Hist.,* (7) XVIII, p. 348 *(Anabas muriei).* Natural Range: From Khartoum, following the White Nile, over the Bahr el Jebel in the area of Lake Albert, Lake Kyoga, Lake Victoria and Lake Edward into the north of Lake Tanganyika. Also westwards into the Chad basin and the bordering regions of the Mayo Kebi basin. (Boulenger, 1906, 1907, 1916; Poll, 1946, 1953; Daget, 1958; Greenwood, 1958; Blache, 1964; Daget and Iltis, 1965; Welcomme, 1969). Ecology: Water holes, ponds

Ctenopoma muriei.

and ditches of swamps near to rivers and lakes; in other words, waters which are left behind after flooding and usually vegetated with grasses and papyrus. The waters are very poor in oxygen. In the area of Lake Edward, *C. damasi* may be found alongside *C. muriei*. Total Length: According to Moerike, female 97mm, male 10mm shorter. Sex Determination: Female more robustly built than male. Male possesses spines behind the eye and at the tail base. Description: Fins: D XIV-XV/7-10, A VIII-X/7-10. Scales: llr 24-28, dlr 13-17/9-14. Captive Care: *C. muriei* is a pretty dull-looking

211

fish and usually only kept by dedicated labyrinth fans. It is recommended that at least 6 fish are kept together in a tank, but other species should be excluded. An aquarium with minimum length of 100cm should be used. Planting is required only for decorative purposes. The foreground should contain a large free-swimming area. All manner of live and dry foods will be taken. There are no special requirements for breeding success. Gravid females are instantly recognizable by their large abdomens. The gravid female is followed by the male and brings his snout to her genital region. It is probable that the female emits a sexually attractive odor and she may sometimes be followed by several males. If not ready to spawn, the female will swim with her head pointed diagonally downwards. When ready to spawn, she will swim in a normal position or with the head pointed diagonally upwards. When ready, she will stop and the male will nod with his head; then the male will grip her in a bodily embrace. The genital openings of the pair come close together. The male's spines play a role in the embrace.

Pairing takes only 2-3 seconds, and the spawning products are released with a shivering of the bodies. The eggs float to the surface. After each spawning act a further one may be started. Males and females will pair indiscriminately. About 2,000 eggs may be laid by a particular female in 1-2 hours. The eggs are clear and yellow tinted; about 0.85mm in diameter. In 24 hours, the fry will hatch and these become free-swimming in another 4 days. They are then about 3mm in length and feed on microscopic life (Rotifera etc.). Special Behavior: This species is a free-spawning labyrinth, which shows no parental care.

Facing page: Top, left *Ctenopoma multispinnis.* Top, right: *Ctenopoma muriei.* Bottom: *Ctenopoma nigropannosum.*

Ctenopoma nanum

Ctenopoma nanum Guenther, 1896. Dwarf Ctenopoma. *nanum* (Lat.) – dwarf. Other Names in the Literature: *Anabas maculatus* (not Thominot) Boulenger, 1882; *Anabas nanus* Boulenger, 1916. First Description: Guenther (1896): *Ann. Mag. Nat. Hist.,* (6) XVII, p. 269. Natural Range: Cameroons and Zaire. Ecology: Fast flowing streams with mineral-poor, soft and clear water. The pH value is between 6 and 6.5. The fish usually hide among roots or overhanging vegetation. Mainly found in rain-forest streams. Total Length: Males about 75mm, females about 10mm shorter. Sex Determination: Male larger with pointed dorsal and anal fins. When excited and during spawning, he shows a dark blue to almost black coloring with no visible pattern. The female is smaller and lighter colored with smaller, rounded fins. Description: Fins: D XV-XVII/7-10, A VII-IX/9-11, C 12. Scales: llr 25-30, dlr 11-18/4-10. In normal coloration, the light brown ground color is broken by darker, cross bands, especially noticeable in the fins. Captive Care: Intra-specific aggression resulting in injuries can occur with this species, so it is recommended to keep them in single pairs, or in a large, well planted tank with adequate refuges. No special requirements with regard to water quality for care or breeding. Water temperature should be maintained between 23 and 25°C. All manner of live and dry foods will be taken. The male builds a bubble nest, usually under a floating leaf if available. During spawning, the female is gripped by the male from beneath and they slowly sink towards the substrate. The spawning products are usually produced as the pair touches the substrate but this may sometimes take place directly under the nest. About 1,000 eggs are produced altogether. These float towards the surface and they are not collected by the male, but are surrounded with bubbles. After each spawning act, the female is driven off. After 24 hours the fry hatch and they hang, tail downwards from the nest. After another 3 days they are free-swimming.

The Dwarf Ctenopoma *Ctenopoma nanum* shown in normal color (top photo) and breeding color (male), lower photo. The males can change colors quickly.

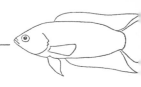

Ctenopoma nigropannosum

Ctenopoma nigropannosum Reichenow, 1875. Two-spot Ctenopoma. Other Names in the Literature: *C. nigrospannosum* Reichenow, 1875; *C. gabonense* Guenther, 1896; *Anabas nigropannosus* Boulenger, 1899. First Description: Reichenow (1875): *Sitzungsb. Ges. Nat. Fr. Berlin,* p. 147. Natural Range: Zaire - in the area of Yangambi (near Kisangani), Gabon and Kongo. Total Length: 170mm (after Boulenger). Sex

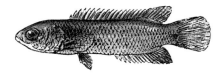

Determination: Only possible by examination of the spines (absent in females). Females are stout when gravid. Description: Fins: D XIX-XX/9-10, A IX/9-10. Scales: llr 30-33, dlr 15-17/12-16. Captive Care: Due to its size and dull coloration, this fish is not often available on the aquaristic market. It is however suitable for large public displays. Special Behavior: This species is very aggressive and unsuitable for community displays. They also show a predilection for

216

jumping out of the tank, so a secure lid is essential. Misc: At first sight, *C. nigropannosum* is very similar in appearance to *Anabas testudineus.*

Ctenopoma ocellatum

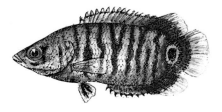

Ctenopoma ocellatum Pellegrin, 1899. Bullseye Ctenopoma, Eye-spot Climbing Perch. *ocellatum* (Lat.) – with an eye spot. Other Names in the Literature: *C. petherici* (not Guenther) Schilthuis, 1891; *C. denticulatum* Pellegrin, 1899; *Anabas weeksii* Boulenger, 1899; *A. ocellatus* Boulenger, 1905; *A. weeksii* Steindachner, 1913; *A. ocellatus* Boulenger, 1916. First Description: Pellegrin (1899): *Bull. Mus. Paris,* p. 359. Natural Range: Congo; Sankuru River, near Kondue, Kasai Province. Ecology: Fast flowing rivers, often near to waterfalls. Sex Determination: Male is slimmer. Exact determination

Above: *Ctenopoma ocellatum*. Photo by Dr. Herbert R. Axelrod of a fish he collected and photographed in the Congo. Below: *Ctenopoma nigropannosum*.

only by examination of spines. Gravid female shows swollen belly. Description: Fins: D XVI-XVIII/9-12, A IX-X/10-12, P 14-15, V I/5, C 17. Scales: llr 26-28, dlr 13-17/7-13. Captive Care: As described for *C. acutirostre.* Misc: Rarely imported. Often confused with *C. acutirostre.*

Ctenopoma oxyrhynchum

Ctenopoma oxyrhynchum (Boulenger, 1902). Mottled Ctenopoma. *oxyrhynchum* (Gr.) – short-snouted. Other Names in the Literature: *Anabas oxyrhynchus* Boulenger, 1902. First Description: Boulenger (1902): *Ann. Mus. Congo, Zool.,* II, p. 52 *(Anabas oxyrhynchus).* Natural Range: Zaire, area of the Ubangi River. Ecology: Slow flowing, clear, mineral poor waters. Total Length: About 110mm. Sex Determination: Outside the spawning season, only by examination of the spines. Gravid females more robustly built. Description: Fins: D XV/10, A VIII/10. Scales: llr 28,

dlr 14-16/9-12. Captive Care: Should be kept in a large tank (min. 100l). Background should be well planted and bogwood provided for hiding places. Feed on the usual mixture of live and dry foods. To promote spawning, small livebearers should be fed to them. No special requirements regarding water quality but a temperature around 23°C is recommended. It is possible to keep this species in community with other species of similar size. For breeding however, it is best to keep this species in single pairs as other tank inmates will eat the eggs. This species usually spawns in the late evening near to the substrate. As soon as spawning occurs, the eggs float to the surface. Altogether about 2,000 eggs are produced. The fry hatch in about 24 hours and are free-swimming in a further 3 days. They may be reared on Rotifera and Cyclops nauplii. The young fish avoid the light and hide under leaves and stones. Special Behavior: It is interesting to note that the light-shy juveniles gather in clusters in suitably dark spots, such as under the leaves of water plants. Where no plants are available, each fish tries to hide under the next. At a length of 20mm, the young fish

Top, right: *Ctenopoma oxyrhynchum* in normal coloration. Top, left: The same fish in spawning dress. Bottom, left: A young *Ctenopoma oxyrhynchum*. Bottom, right: The typical mouth-stretching for which this group is noted.

219

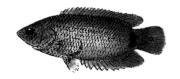

show a very dark pattern which weakens as they grow larger, eventually becoming light brown. A typical characteristic is the dark eye spot on the center of the body; but even this disappears during spawning. Misc: In spawning colors, this species is very similar in appearance to *C. maculatum*. Use a fine meshed net for catching up these fish, otherwise they will become entangled in the mesh with their spines and the net will have to be cut if they are to be released without injury.

Ctenopoma pellegrini

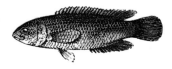

Ctenopoma pellegrini (Boulenger, 1902). *pellegrini* – after Pellegrin. First Description: Boulenger (1902): *Ann. Mus. Congo. Zool.*, II, p. 51. Natural Range: After Boulenger: Zaire in the Ubangi River area. Total Length: 105mm (Boulenger). Description: Fins: D XVIII-XIX/10-11, A VII/10. Scales: llr 33-34, dlr 16-18/14-15. Captive Care: No information available. Misc: Very similar to

C. nigropannosum and, until more research is carried out, it cannot be ruled out that this is not one and the same species.

Ctenopoma petherici

Ctenopoma petherici Guenther, 1864. *petherici* - after Petherick. Other Names in the Literature: *Anabas petherici*. Boulenger, 1899. First Description: Guenther (1864): *Ann. Mag. Nat. Hist.*, (3) XIII, p. 211. Natural Range: White Nile, Bahr el Gebel, Lake Chad (after Boulenger). Total Length: 160mm (Boulenger). Description: D XVII-XIX/8-10, A X/10-11. Scales: llr 28-30, dlr 14-17/10-12.

In addition, the following species are mentioned in the literature but are so far unknown in the aquarium: *C. breviventralis* Pellegrin, 1938; *C. brunneum* (Ahl,1927); *C. caudomaculatum* (Ahl, 1927); *C. davidae* Poll, 1939; *C. garuanum* (Ahl, 1927); *C. machadoi* Fowler, 1938; *C. pekkolai* Rendahl, 1935; *C.*

riggenbachi (Ahl, 1927); *C. vermayi* Fowler, 1935.

The following species is known from just one specimen and is, so far, of little importance to the aquarist

Genus *Oshimia* Jordan, 1919. Number of Species: 1. Size: 45mm. Shape: Elongate. Fin Formation: medium ventrals (I/5), 3 hard and 7 soft dorsal rays, 4 hard and 23 soft anal rays.

Oshimia marchei

Oshimia marchei (Sauvage, 1878). Other Names in the Literature: *Micracanthus marchei* Sauvage, 1878; *M. marchii* Boulenger, 1916; *Oshimia marchii* Jordan, 1919. First Description: Sauvage (1878): *Bull. Soc. Philom. Paris*, (7) III, pp. 95/96 (*Micracanthus marchei*) Natural Range: Collected in Province Doume in the Ogowe River area (Gabon). Total Length: 45mm. Description: Fins: D III/7, A IV/23, V I/5. Scales: llr 35, dlr 9. Large comb scales; uniform brown in color. No opercular scales.

A typical swamp habitat of *Betta imbellis*, *Betta pugnax* and *Trichopsis vittatus*. Photo by Horst Linke.

221

Index